RORY

Design and Layout: Scott Giarnese

Publishers: Jules Gammond & Alan Jones for G2 Entertainment Ltd.

Picture Credits: FlickR (supergolfdude, zzazazz, kompuder_dude)
ShutterStock

The right of Justin Doyle to be identified as the author of this book has been
asserted by them in accordance with the Copyright, Designs and Patents Act
1988.

Printed and bound by CPI Group (UK) Ltd, Croydon, CR0 4YY

ISBN: 978-1-908461-92-6

RORY
His Story So Far

Written by
Justin Doyle

Foreword
Gary Player

G2 entertainment

Contents

Foreword

Professional golfers who today 'burst on to the scene' at a young age face very different challenges to those we faced when I won my first Major, the Open Championship, at Muirfield in 1959, at the age of 23.

At that time, we had to win to earn a living and support our families. There were no private jets, no multi-million dollar purses, no 24-hour news and sports channels and no social media, and the golf press was a small, dedicated group.

In those days, golf journalists wrote passionately about the game, with no salacious details about the players' personal lives. It is a very different planet we live on today.

To become a world champion you need to practise harder than everyone else, and you need to dedicate yourself to improving every week. Your mind and body have to be capable of peak performance, and that takes time, sacrifice and serious effort.

Rising stars like Rory are now faced with figuring out how to balance these needs amid constant media coverage and celebrity. Most importantly, he must find out how to avoid complacency and settling for winning only once in a while.

Rory clearly has tremendous talent and ability. Winning the US Open at the age of 21 was an incredible feat in itself, and doing so in such a dominant manner was even more impressive.

Coming back to win a Major championship after such a difficult experience at the Masters shows us that he has a strong mind. Being mentally strong is one thing, but does he have what it takes to become only the sixth man ever to win the Grand Slam?

That is yet to be seen, but as I told him the day after he won his first Major, I for one truly believe he can do it.

Golf is a fantastic sport that has provided me with a life that I only dreamt about when I realised I truly loved the game and wanted to become a world champion. That was the key for me: deciding I wanted to be the best.

It is a mindset. It is an essential and firm belief in oneself combined with a burning desire and passion to win. And most importantly, that mindset also contains the willingness to make the personal sacrifices necessary to achieve this type of success.

When you see a young man like Rory, with the talent of Jack Nicklaus and the passion of Tiger Woods and who represents himself, his family, his country and his sport in the style he does, you know he has the ability to become a special player.

You also know that in today's world he will have to face intense pressure and scrutiny.

Rory, YOU have the game, now go out and show yourself and the world that YOU have the desire. Remember, 'the harder you practise, the luckier you get'.

My very best wishes to you,

Gary Player

Introduction

If you travel through the Northern Ireland capital of Belfast, then past the newly named George Best International Airport and the old Harland & Wolff shipyard on your left, you will come to the small borough of Holywood on your right-hand side.

Situated in the north-east of the city, the area could be missed so easily. If it wasn't for the fact that you were going in search of it, you could be forgiven for thinking that it was just a part of the Belfast suburbs.

A small sign on a grassy knoll proclaims that you are in Holywood, but there is no glitz, glamour or razzamatazz here. Life in this part of the world is quiet and peaceful, light years away from its near namesake in California.

In fact, it is hard to believe that, just seven or eight minutes' drive from the hustle and bustle of the city centre, you can arrive at such an oasis of calm. For Holywood is exactly that: it is an area of such greenery, such beauty and such tranquility.

At the other end of the town, a 500 metre walk uphill from Holywood's main street and shopping area, you arrive at Glenlyon. This is a picnic area and lay-by surrounded and shaded by tall trees. And when you take a stroll through the area, it soon becomes obvious how this town got its name, for amid the trees and plants of every type, size and colour, holly trees are abundant.

Everything and everybody seems so relaxed in this Holywood. Even the golf club, nestled on a height overlooking Belfast Lough, is untypically serene. There are no eager golfers scurrying to make tee times nor the noisy pop of golf shots.

The placidity hides a course that is quite restrictive and confined, as well as very hilly. It is tough. But these are the very fairways where several generations of McIlroys have strolled in pursuit of their love of golf.

Rory McIlroy is Belfast through and through. Everything about the city is in his body and soul. Belfast is his blood, flesh and bones and it is in his accent, his mannerisms and his thought processes. But the characteristics of Holywood are in his DNA.

Rory is not just a cog in the Belfast wheel – he is the very fabric of it. His family is woven from Belfast cloth. In a province that gave the world flax and so many weavers, Rory's blood can be said to be one of the very first dyes running through that cloth.

When you pass those imposing Harland & Wolff cranes, you are also reminded that this is the area that helped bring Rory into the world. The site that produced the *Titanic* would, almost exactly a century later, launch Rory to the top of the golf world.

That is no exaggeration. It is stone cold fact. For Rory's grandfather, Jimmy McIlroy, worked all the hours God gave him to put bread on the table for his family, through endless shifts and long hours repairing those famous cranes on the docks of Belfast. And Jimmy did not just repair them; he kept them well oiled and in great working condition. Just as today's workers keep modern aircraft and airbuses ticking over and in pristine condition, there was huge responsibility placed on him.

The docks that Jimmy worked on are reputed to be the exact same ones where the infamous *Titanic* was built at the turn of the last century. Many more of the world's biggest passenger liners and ships were rolled out to the world from there. Times were hard, but the steady work helped Jimmy raise three sons – Colm, Brian and Gerry, the last of whom was born in October 1959. In later life, Gerry met and married Rosie and the hard work ethic on which they were both brought up continued to be a major force in their lives.

They raised a family together and, on Thursday, 4 May 1989, Rosie gave birth to Rory, who was later baptised at St Patrick's Church in Holywood. Soon after, Rosie returned to making ends meet, working in the 3M factory in Belfast.

When the young Rory was old enough to attend school, and Gerry was out working during the day, Rosie slept. Then, when Gerry was at home in their small, red-brick council house and taking care of Rory, Rosie worked through the night. In the little spare time she had to herself, Rosie loved to knit, and when time permitted, Gerry was able to play a little more golf with his two brothers and father at Holywood Golf Club, where he developed a great love for the game.

But aside from golf and hard work, life was far from plain sailing in Northern Ireland back then. As teenagers and adolescents growing up in the mid-1970s and 1980s, Gerry and Rosie lived through the worst of the Troubles. And living and working in Holywood did not mean they were immune from it all. As beautiful as the area is, it is not so far from the city centre and very few places, if any, escaped those brutal times.

Belfast fared worst of all and the McIlroys and their extended families did not escape the horrors of that terrible period in Northern Ireland's history. In July 2011, detectives reopened the case of the unsolved murder of Joseph McIlroy. The family have never spoken of this tragedy and continue to maintain a dignified silence.

Joe, who was only 30 years old when he died, was a computer technician and the uncle of Rory's father, Gerry. He lived with his wife Mary and their four young daughters on a smart middle-class housing estate in a Protestant area of East Belfast. They had lived there for four years and had already experienced attacks and abuse.

Then, on 21 November 1972, two Ulster Volunteer Force gunmen hid in their back garden. According to police files, the men wore rubber-soled shoes to avoid being heard as they crept up to the kitchen window. Joe was killed by a volley of shots fired through that window.

What made the killing all the more harrowing for the McIlroys, and all hard-working decent people, was the fact that he was murdered while working to fix a kitchen appliance.

But life went on and Rory's parents began to notice that the toddler seemed to have a very special gift. Gerry was amazed one day to see young Rory do things while playing with plastic, bendy golf clubs that a normal kid – even an adult – could not. It was not so much that Rory could hit a ball a relatively long way with such a basic golf club; it was a lot more than that. There was something very striking and remarkable about the way he held and swung that club.

Look back now at that home-made video footage of Rory striking golf balls between the ages of three and four and you will see what Gerry and Rosie saw. This young boy was a God-send. There was no doubt he had something very special.

Looking at the footage is eerie, to the point that you are left wondering if this is really a former great golfer reincarnated in the body of a toddler – a Ben Hogan, a Francis Ouimet or a Harry Vardon, perhaps. Early videos of David Beckham or Stephen Hendry pale by comparison.

Gerry McIlroy knew he had to harness his son's talent – and quickly. As golfers themselves, he and his brothers knew they had in young Rory a golfer with infinitely more potential and skill than they had ever had.

To help pave the way for his young son to become a golfer, and to give him every chance to nurture his talents, Gerry cleaned lockers at a local rugby club in the mornings and worked as a barman during the afternoons and nights. The hours were gruelling. He put in over 100 hours a week but he believed all the effort was worthwhile because he trusted wholeheartedly in his instincts; because he knew what Rory possessed.

Gerry purchased a little red golf bag for Rory, and cut some clubs down to suit his size. Rosie knitted a pink sweater and bought a small pair of black waterproofs to help protect him from the wind and rain.

It was surreal to see a two-year-old toddler walking alongside his father with his little golf bag, and striking the ball with small fairway woods cut to size. Golfers were scratching their heads at what they had witnessed.

Here was a mere baby, decked out in golf gear and walking the golf course with a golf bag and a caddy. More to the point, here was a baby who struck the ball like no other baby the world had ever seen.

Enjoy reading through the next twenty-one years of Rory McIlroy's life.

Chapter 1:
A Master in Waiting

Upstairs in the clubhouse at Holywood Golf Club are two framed pictures that catch the eye. One is a framed print of Rory McIlroy posing proudly with the trophy of his first European title, the Dubai Desert Classic. Next to it, on the right, is a much more colourful and larger frame. In the top half of the frame, a yellow flag is set. It is from the US Masters at Augusta. It is signed by Rory, and the reason it is there becomes apparent when one looks at the photo below it.

In a mass of green Georgia fairway, a small, distant Rory McIlroy is photographed watching the flight of his ball towards the green from his follow-through swing. The image is utterly captivating and expressive.

An art connoisseur's train of thought might be that the golfer, the ball and the green are all so small while, in contrast, the Augusta Masters, the fairway and the bunkers are so large – even larger than still life! Whatever one's interpretation of the picture, the fact is that the scene is based on one of Augusta's most famous holes, 'Azalea'.

The 13th hole is named after the exotic flowers that bloom everywhere on the famous course. That is where the beauty ends. In the bright light of reality, this is one of the most difficult holes in the world of golf. It is also one of the most treacherous par fives, filled with traps and pitfalls, that any golfer could ever encounter.

As is the nature of a par five, Azalea does yield plenty of birdies. But every year it also serves up more bogeys than the rest of the par fives, and nothing is ever easy or taken for granted when playing this hole. This is how a golf manual describes it: "A risk reward hole full of danger. Rae's Creek (out of bounds) runs down the side and across the front of the green, while there are four bunkers over the back, making birdies anything but routine for those failing to find the putting surface."

On his first visit to play in the US Masters, in 2009, Rory got a nice feel for the tough course during his first round and finished on level par, 72. The next day, he eagled that infamous 13th after his second shot finished six feet from the pin.

The events of that feat, of that moment, are captured in the frame that has been hanging proudly on the wall in Holywood Golf Club ever since. In essence, it is a small trophy brought back from a famous battle.

There were to be a lot more skirmishes in that round. After his magnificent eagle, Rory succumbed by bogeying the par four 14th but fought back to get a birdie on the very next, a par five. But by the end, there were scars and a bitter taste in his mouth: he double-bogeyed the par three 16th and then triple-bogeyed the par four 18th.

For many golfers, that would have spelt the end. However, Rory still finished his round in 73, one over par, and he made the cut in his very first Masters.

At 19 years of age and one of only three teenagers in the field, along with 17-year-old Ryo Ishikawa and 18-year-old Danny Lee, Rory was beginning to win many admirers for his tenaciousness. Andy Farrell of the *Independent* wrote: "What makes Rory McIlroy so good? He could be the definition of an old head on a young body. The latter gives him a power game with a solid technique, the former a maturity beyond his years. But it does not matter how young or experienced you are, a triple bogey at the last hole still tastes like dirt.

"On the leaderboard one minute, McIlroy dropped five strokes in the last three holes, with a double-bogey at the short 16th and a seven to finish. McIlroy comes across as experienced beyond his years but some experiences just have to be taken on the chin. He signed for a 73 to be one over par, on the cut line."

However, although he had made it into the weekend, the first real controversial moment of Rory's fledgling professional career then ensued. BBC television shocked the watching millions by announcing that he was on the verge of disqualification!

In running up the triple-bogey seven at the 18th that relegated him from being up on the leaderboard at two under par to just surviving the cut at one over, he showed frustration and anger, as Brian Keogh of the *Sun* explained in his Tweet from the course: "Bunkered in the right greenside trap at the 18th, he failed to escape with his first attempt and angrily kicked at the sand before semi-shanking his fourth shot across to the green from where he took three putts.

"Kicking the sand could be considered 'testing the condition of a hazard' under rule 13-4, bringing with it a two-stroke penalty and subsequent disqualification for signing for an incorrect score."

A typically nonchalant and unfussed McIlroy took it all in his stride. After watching replays of the incident, he told the BBC that he felt he had done no wrong. To survive Augusta only to be disqualified would have been a cruel end to a Masters debut. But like a jockey facing a steward's enquiry, he had to accept whatever fate the officials bestowed on him. As Rory held his hand up admitting he was at the mercy of 'The Rules', the officials were in their cabin deliberating. Everyone waited nervously.

After almost three hours of examining and discussing the incident, the committee cleared McIlroy of any wrongdoing or infringement of the rules. The relief probably took away from the disappointing end to his round, and it actually spurred Rory on.

His resilience and courage were once again displayed for all to see during the last two rounds. On the third day, he rose to a -1 round of 71 that included his making par at every single hole on the back nine, including its notorious Amen Corner.

The skirmishes continued but Rory won out. After a shaky start, his final round was magnificent overall. After parring every one of the last nine holes the previous day, he birdied six of the last ten holes in his final round and parred the other four. It was the sort of play we have come to expect from Tiger Woods in recent years and Rory finished in a tie for 20th position in his maiden Masters. At two under par, he had beaten Augusta.

In an article by Emily Benammar in the *Telegraph* a few days after that 2009 Masters, South African golf legend Gary Player could not hide his admiration for McIlroy. Himself a winner of three Masters green jackets, Player, who also made a record 52nd and final appearance at that tournament, described McIlroy's swing as "unbelievable". He said: "Rory McIlroy, if he goes about it and is managed correctly, could turn out to be the best player in the world in his time. This young man is brilliant. His golf swing is unbelievable and his theory side, his swing, is better than Tiger Woods.

"He's an incredible talent and has excelled already at a very young age. I believe he's a very nice young man too and I hope he goes from strength to strength."

After such an eventful Masters debut in 2009, Rory returned to Georgia the following year only to suffer the dreadful disappointment of missing the cut. It was a huge blow for him and especially for his growing legions of followers. With great players like Fred Couples and Tiger having fantastic records of making many, many consecutive cuts at Augusta, for Rory to miss the mark in his second Masters was something of an embarrassment.

However, there seems to have been a legitimate excuse. In late January 2010 and into early February, McIlroy was troubled by a deep-seated back injury. It plagued him during his defence of the Dubai Desert Classic and it was the cause of his dip in form.

He actually started his Masters first round very well with a birdie at the short par four third hole, but that is really as good as it got. Four bogeys followed and, although he birdied the 14th, he signed his card for a two-over par 74.

Things got even worse the next day as six straight pars were followed by a double-bogey at the seventh and a bogey at the eighth. Two more bogeys coming home meant Rory finished his round with a disastrous 77, five over par, and he was on his way home.

Fed up and dejected, he immediately announced he was taking a six-week break from the game. There were some who argued that he was suffering more mental than physical problems. But McIlroy felt he needed time out, as he explained in the *Belfast Telegraph*. "I just didn't play well and I need a bit of time to get it back on track," he said.

"I don't know what is going on, I just need to take a bit of a break and come back with a refreshed attitude. I am getting frustrated very easily and getting down on myself. I just think that I need to go home and get my head sorted. I am supposed to play Quail Hollow (on the US Tour) in a couple of weeks, but I might need a bit more time to let this injury clear up and clear my head. Maybe I'll come back at Wentworth (May 20-23) or something."

Rory added: "We will see what happens. The back is okay. I can still feel it, but if I rest it then it will be fine. I don't think this is due to the expectation on me. I have done all of these great things myself so a lot of that expectation is from myself. Maybe I just need to sit down and tell myself that I am only 20 years old and that things are actually going well for me. I have felt this down before – probably the summer of 2008 – but all it takes is one good week and you can be back up there."

****

In April 2011, Rory returned to Augusta fresh and fighting fit, having played just five events since the start of the season. Of the world's top 20 golfers, only Luke Donald, with four, had played fewer – but Phil Mickelson had made the cut in all nine he had played.

Rory, at world number nine, was in good form entering his third Masters. He had made the cut in the five events he had played, and after a magnificent second place on his seasonal bow in Abu Dhabi, he had also had two top ten finishes, in Dubai and at the World Golf Championships.

There was, however, one niggling statistic that was just a little bit worrying. Although he had finished tenth on his last outing at the WGC in Florida, Rory's two previous performances in the US had been far from impressive. He had failed to reach the quarter-final stage at the World Matchplay in Arizona, won by Donald. For sure, it was Matchplay, but at the Honda Classic in Florida following that, he could only finish the week in 70th position.

Three of his four previous visits to the American southern states had left a lot to be desired. Rory had questions to answer, and not the least of them was the fact that a year earlier at Augusta, he had failed to make the cut.

So there were actually no great expectations about McIlroy's chances going into Augusta, and that was also the case with the other two Irish golfers. Padraig Harrington was way out of form and struggling while Graeme McDowell had missed the cut at Bay Hill.

In an interview with the *Irish Times* on the weekend before the Masters, legendary coach Butch Harmon said McIlroy would not win the Masters until his short game improved. Harmon, who has coached Woods and Mickelson, said: "Rory hits the ball from right to left, so that's the good news, but I'm not sure his short game is of the quality of some of the other players."

But despite his misgivings over McIlroy's putting, Harmon did predict that the Ulsterman would one day triumph at Augusta, adding: "Rory is a great talent and should one day be a Masters champion."

On Tuesday, April 5, two days before the event got under way, the pairings and tee times were announced. For the first two days Rory was paired with Rickie Fowler of the US and Jason Day of Australia. Fowler, who played on the losing American team against Rory's Europe in the 2010 Ryder Cup, is recognised as one of America's young pretenders and a future star. Day would eventually end up playing with Rory every day for the first three days.

At 9.24 on Thursday morning, Holywood's finest teed off for what would become a dream start. He made birdies at the par five second, par four third, par three fourth and par four ninth to be out in four under par – just 31 shots with no bogeys. Further birdies at 11, 14 and 15 and no dropped shots meant Rory finished a fantastic round at seven under par. All around the world, from Brisbane to Buenos Aires, the wires proclaimed young Irishman Rory McIlroy leading the US Masters, albeit as joint leader with Spain's Alvaro Quiros.

After his magnificent round, Rory spoke to the world's press. To one reporter, he spoke of the relief he had felt at making up for his missed cut at Augusta the previous year when he said: "It's a great start to the tournament but obviously there is still a long way to go.

But I'm just glad I got that little monkey off my back."

In the seven rounds he had played at Augusta, this was the very first time he had hit a round in the 60s. He had also become the youngest player to lead the Masters since Seve Ballesteros, who was 23 when he led in 1980.

It was a round of sheer perfection and unbridled joy and a privilege for golf fans everywhere to watch. It was also a major triumph to wipe out the memories of the double bogey and triple bogey at the 16th and 18th in 2009 and his 77 in 2010.

The next day, Rory had an afternoon tee-off time. He set out at 12.42 and by the time he came back in, he had a two-shot lead over his playing partner Jason Day. His four birdies in a round of 69 were spoiled by his very first bogey on the 12th.

Rory McIlroy was two shots clear of the field after the second round of the US Masters. This is what Larry Dorman of the *New York Times* wrote: "With rosy cheeks that appear in no need of shaving and a shock of curly, brown hair that cascades from beneath his cap, McIlroy could easily pass for a high school kid and, at times, would just as soon act like one.

"Take the night this week at one of the better addresses in a staid Augusta neighbourhood. It was the eve of the season's first major championship, the most awaited event of the year here and annually the golf tournament watched by more people worldwide than any other.

"So what was the kid from Holywood, Northern Ireland, up to? Whooping it up under the lights, trying to do a Tom Brady impression in the cul-de-sac, passing a football around with his Holywood buddies Harry Diamond, Rickey McCormick and Harry Tweedie. 'Sort of got into American football from being over here and just wanted to learn how to throw it a little bit better,' McIlroy said. 'Bought a football, threw it around a little bit. Yeah, I was actually told off by the lady living across the street. We were making a bit too much noise. Had to cut it short.'

"McIlroy has been making a lot of noise for a long time on golf courses around the world, and now he leads the Masters after two rounds. From the first time he belted a ball 40 yards as a three-year-old, he had 'star' written all over him. It will be written larger if he can continue to do what he has done for the past two days at the Augusta National GC.

"Regardless of the outcome here, McIlroy will deal with it down the road. Along with the carefree spirit he has been manifesting this week, there are a maturity and perspective that are years beyond his age."

Rory was enjoying every minute of his third Masters. His dreams of winning it were now steadily becoming a reality. But quite aside from the golf, the camaraderie among his fellow golfers was very pleasing, and it was helping to keep him focused. He enjoyed great banter with both playing partners, Fowler and Day. McIlroy could be seen laughing, smiling and having an all-round good time. They even applauded each other's shots. When he was asked what all the fun was about, Rory remarked that all three talked about anything and everything. In particular, he said, they talked about fast cars and boats!

In his third round, Rory again began well. After parring the first three holes, he birdied the par three fourth to move to 11 under par. Two bogeys followed before he closed with three more birdies in his last six holes.

This meant that Rory was on -12 going into the final round. He had also increased his lead over the rest of the field to four shots. It was the biggest final round lead since Tiger Woods had led by nine shots in 1997.

On Sunday, Rory would be in the final pairing with Argentina's Angel Cabrera, who was seeking his second Masters. The omens were good for Rory as the vast majority of previous winners had all come from the last pairing.

When he faced the media after his penultimate round, Rory was still in high spirits. He was relaxed and he revealed even more golfing camaraderie. To the amusement of reporters, he stated he had just received a text from Graeme McDowell: "He just texted me and told me he loved me. I don't know what that means. I don't know if that's him or the beer talking!"

****

Ireland is a sports-mad nation. When one of their own is involved at the business end of a major sporting event, every man, woman and child in the country is transfixed by the event. The dogs and cats are thrown out in case they make a noise. In homes, a bottle or two is uncorked while in every corner of the land the pubs, clubs and hotels are packed, with every eye fixed on the small screen and every hand on a pint glass. So pull up a seat and let us join Rory in his final round.

****

Dwarfed by playing partner Cabrera, who looks like his frame could accommodate three McIlroys, Rory steps forward to tee off. Understandably, he looks a little nervous but he shakes off the nerves to unleash a perfect drive on the tough first hole, named Tea Olive.

He makes a beautiful connection with his second, but then something in his facial expression says he feels something is not right. When the ball lands on the green, it kicks away to the left. He drops a shot. It is a nervy start, and another calamity awaits.

On the par five second, Rory drives into a bunker. With his second shot he hits the lip of the sand trap. Hands are in heads. There are nervous looks on faces throughout Ireland. Rory must be feeling pretty lonely and his heart must be thumping.

His third shot goes into the bunker. He plays a great recovery from the sand and scrambles home the putt for par. Surely that will help to steady the nerves. In any case, the third, Flowering Peach, is up next, and it is a very makeable birdie hole.

Rory hits a 3-wood right up the centre of the fairway and then plays a majestic iron shot to six feet. That is more like Rory. In Lavery's in Belfast, the packed bar must be cheering. The groans tell you he misses the birdie chance. And it is a very bad miss.

A safe iron into the par three fourth means a long outside birdie chance. Two putts means he settles for par. Things are not getting any easier. Nothing is happening for him, while up ahead the crowds are hollering as Charl Swartzel is holing everything.

At Magnolia, the par four fifth hole, Rory again drives brilliantly, but a poor approach puts him under pressure. A great chip to around seven feet must surely secure a par. But a poor putt has entire pubs in Kilburn, north London cursing the fates.

Rory must be starting to feel that destiny is rapidly turning against him. A weak iron shot into Juniper, the par three sixth, means that he just accepts another two putts for par. Even Cabrera is now looking a more likely winner.

By now, a new expression has appeared on Rory's face. It signals that he has had enough of this messing about. He can hear them in Donegal's Mount Errigal Hotel shouting in their Northern drawl: "Catch yerself on."

His best drive of the day sets up his first birdie from around 15 feet. The smile is back and the adrenalin is running again. Hold on … maybe a little too much as two huge hits on the par five eighth see his ball run through the green. He settles for par.

At the halfway mark, on the par four ninth, Rory unleashes another monster drive. His driving has been a revelation today; it's his putting that has let him down. It does so again as another great birdie chance slides past.

With Cabrera, as well as Schwartzel up ahead, playing excellent golf, it is now all change at the top. Rory must have promised himself over and over again not to look up at the leaderboard, no matter what was unfolding around him. It is so hard. A voice in his head tells him to look up for just a second. He glances up and his heart surely sinks. Schwartzel, Cabrera, Choi and Woods are now ganging up on him, all ten under par. From four ahead, he is just a shaky shot in front.

Then the ultimate disaster strikes. Rory's drive on the tenth clips a tree and ricochets into the garden of a neighbouring house. It is possible that the sheer embarrassment of being in there, allied to everything else going wrong, forced him to hit another tree.

He ends up with a triple-bogey seven. From a shot in front, he is now two shots behind at eight under. It is sad viewing. Television sets are switched off in their tens of thousands. In Doran's, off Fifth Avenue in New York, the bartender pours himself a drink.

Things get even worse. After playing two great shots into the 11th green, Rory's mind must be in turmoil after that tenth hole, and it takes him three putts to get down. It is yet another bogey and he falls further back, to seven under par.

Sitting room lights are now switched off and it is time for bed. It is safe to say that hundreds of thousands of people go to their beds with heavy hearts. Watching a young and talented golfer capitulate like this is akin to watching a horror movie.

Even then, the cruelty is not spared. Safely on the 12th green, he four-putts for bogey. End of story, over and out. If it was hard for most people to watch and stomach, we cannot even begin to think how it was for Rory.

There is no point in recording the last six holes; it does not make any better reading. Rory must have given up. Not that he wanted to; it's just that his head must have been a mess. How could he see straight, never mind hit straight?

After making a 147 maximum break some years ago, snooker great Stephen Hendry said he didn't know how he had held his cue straight. The nervous tension was such that he could hear his heart beating in his ears and his legs felt like jelly. Rory must surely have experienced that in a converse way. He must have felt the same way Jimmy White did as the 'Whirlwind' watched big leads and world snooker titles disappear down through the years.

At the 18th, after an ugly 80, it was all over. Rory had dropped from 12 under all the way down to -4. In fact, it is doubtful that Rory knew what scores he was racking up over those closing holes. He probably did not even know who was winning the Masters.

It was time to get away. The media would have to wait. Pain, frustration and the feeling of embarrassment played out in front of his family, friends and multitudes of Irish, had to be dealt with in only one way – floods of tears at the end of a sad day.

****

Following his Masters debacle, now euphemistically referred to as 'Rory's Masters meltdown', he dusted himself down and, after composing himself, spoke to American television reporters. Visibly ashen-faced, he said: "I'm very disappointed at the minute and I'm sure I will be for the next few days, but I'll get over it. I have to take the positives and the positives are I led this golf tournament for 63 holes." He added: "I'll have plenty more chances, I know that. It's very disappointing what happened today and hopefully it will build a little bit of character in me as well."

At that moment he did not know it, but he had just won himself millions of fans all over the world for his bravery, modesty and dignity in his very gracious acceptance of defeat. Later, commentators drew comparisons between the way in which he had conducted himself and some of Tiger Woods' 'losing' interviews.

For the next few days and weeks, while the print and broadcast media speculated and pored over Rory's collapse, he took time out to get away from it all. The fact is, in that simple interview Rory gave, he was showing that he is only human.

The media will always continue to analyse, and even sensationalise, but there is really no secret and nothing new in his collapse. Rory was not the first and he certainly will not be the last to suffer such a cruel end to a major.

Australian Greg Norman suffered an even bigger disaster. In the 1996 Masters, the Great White Shark went into the final round with a six-stroke lead over England's Nick Faldo – and he ended up losing the title to Faldo by five shots.

In sport, nothing is ever guaranteed. As the saying goes, it ain't over until the fat lady sings. Big leads are lost for three main reasons: pressure, fatigue and fate. Perhaps with Greg it was pressure and for Rory, maybe a little piece of all three.

The first of those Rory encountered was fate. He probably knew from the ninth hole that he was destined not to win, which is why he threw caution to the wind over the next few holes, with disastrous consequences.

However, he actually showed signs very early in the round that he was not happy with the cards he was being dealt. His ball hitting the green on the first and then bouncing wickedly to the left, from where he then made bogey, was a bitter pill to swallow. Clipping the lip of the bunker, finding sand and missing several makeable putts was also very hard to take.

There is also a very strong case to be made for fatigue playing a big part in his demise. 'Wire-to-wire' is a term used in the US when someone, in sport, leads from start to finish. In golf, it is very hard to do. Golf statistics throw up very few winners who have led on all four days – and the signs were there for Rory not becoming one of the very rare 'all the way' winners. The evidence points to his regressing on each of the three days prior to his collapse: he had hit rounds of 67, 69, 70 before that terrible 80.

There are many who will say that it is the pressure that does this. That is possible. But it is more likely to be physical and mental fatigue that are the relevant factors. It is like a horse going out in front early on in the Grand National: everyone knows that horse will not win.

Pressure on the other hand, brings in many characteristics all of its own, and intimidation is one. Rory could have felt intimidated by his playing partner, Angel Cabrera. The sheer size of the man; the monster drives on just a three-quarter swing; his relaxed manner and the ease with which he made his birdies to close within one shot of Rory. All of this could have piled the pressure on the young man.

Noise is another possible factor. The cacophony of the euphoric celebrations all around the course could have shocked and alarmed him, and Rory would no doubt have been wondering what was happening in the groups ahead of him. As Schwartzel, KJ Choi, Woods, Cabrera and Bo Van Pelt all made outrageous birdies and eagles, Rory would undoubtedly have felt under pressure to do something himself. As it was, he was desperately trying to make things happen.

We can all only speculate and wonder. The fact is that whatever Rory felt, he will most likely never reveal it until his career is over. No golfer ever will. To do so would only give opponents an opportunity to exploit any weakness in future events and majors.

McIlroy did, however, give a very strong hint that perhaps pressure was the number one reason for what happened. In those very words he spoke afterwards, he ended with: " … hopefully it will build a little bit of character in me."

After all, it is not losing that is going to build a little character in a golfer; it is learning how to deal with the way he loses. Most importantly, it is learning how to deal with everything thrown at him on the day of the loss – bad luck, pressure, fatigue.

Every competitor in every sport has to deal with it, and some deal with it better than others. A true champion stands on a pedestal above the rest. He or she shows enough fortitude, skill and courage in situations of duress to overcome every obstacle and triumph.

After the US Masters, the big question was: could Rory bounce back?

Chapter 2:
Time for Congress

Rory McIlroy took his time in coming back, spending almost two months away from the States. He actually made his return just two weeks before the second major of the year, at Muirfield Village's Memorial Tournament in Dublin, Ohio.

In fact, he did not make his return in Europe until May 19, when he played the World Matchplay in Spain. He beat Retief Goosen in the first round but then lost to Nicolas Colsaerts. The following week he finished three over par at the BMW in Wentworth.

So coming into the Memorial, his form was poor. But after shooting a first round 66, it seemed as if his batteries were becoming fully charged, especially as he sat proudly on top of the leaderboard with American Chris Riley.

It was probably too much, too early to expect fireworks and, over the following two days, he never really looked like winning. Steve Stricker, in scintillating form, was the only player in the field to record four successive under-par rounds. He won with rounds of 68, 67, 69 and 68 and ended up a rare wire-to-wire winner.

Rory's 66, 72, 71 and 68 left him five shots adrift of the American, and he finished fifth. But he was the leading European, with a two-shot advantage over Luke Donald. On the whole, he was delighted with how everything had gone, as he told *Sky Sports*: "I played really good this week. I just made a few too many mistakes, which really cost me. We'll have to try and cut those out before the US Open in two weeks' time. But there are definitely a lot of positives to take from how I've played. I putted the ball really good and that's a huge positive to take into the US Open. Everything is pretty good."

He also showed maturity way beyond his years, as well as a willingness to learn and do his homework, as he added: "I just need a little bit of strategy more than anything else. If you're going to miss shots, miss them in the right places. If you miss greens it's very penal here and you get punished quite easily. It's the same as the US Open. If you miss it in the wrong places there, you're looking at a five or a six. So it's just something I need to address a little bit."

In 2009, Rory played in his first US Open at Bethpage Black, in his second appearance in a US major following his efforts in the Masters a few months previously. On a tough par 70 course, he shot rounds of 72/70/72 to be four over entering the final round. Lucas Glover surged clear on the last day to win the title on -4, two shots clear of Phil Mickelson, Ricky Barnes and a back-to-form David Duval. Rory shot a great final round of 68 to finish in a tie for tenth at two over par.

But 2010 turned out to be a year to forget for Rory in the United States. He missed the cut at the so-called 'fifth major', the Players Championship; again at the US Masters; and then at the US Open.

While his good friend Graeme McDowell went on to win his first major in that US Open in Pebble Beach, with a level par score of 284, Rory went out of the event very tamely. Rounds of 75 and 77 meant he finished the tournament at ten over par.

Just before the 2011 US Open, McIlroy underwent a life-changing experience. A few days in advance of the second major, he visited earthquake-hit Haiti in his capacity as a UNICEF Ireland Ambassador, a role he had taken up in March. During his visit to Haiti, he met pupils from a school that had been destroyed by the 2010 earthquake and, among other things, learned how pupils are now educated to protect themselves from cholera. He also saw at first hand how they are picking up the pieces and learning to fend for themselves.

As he left the region and returned to his US base, he was informed that a further 20 people had been killed in floods and landslides. It clearly had an effect on him and he acknowledged this on his website. Earlier, an emotional McIlroy had said: "The chance that these kids are getting – to be kids and to enjoy themselves – is so important for their well-being. Nothing could prepare me for meeting the children in Haiti and I am truly amazed by how happy they are. The everyday things that we take for granted back home in Ireland are so longed for in Haiti."

The experience made him realise what his talent had afforded him. However, on his way to Congressional for the Open, he could not shake the images and experiences of that visit to Haiti out of his mind. He said: "You know, Haiti made me realise there really is more to life than golf. It has instilled in me a feeling that the next time I struggle on the golf course or whatever, I'll think of the people of Haiti. That will change my mindset pretty quickly."

Perhaps it would even help inspire him to try that little bit harder to win his first major. The fact is, when he talked about his innermost feelings concerning his trip to Haiti, it no doubt put his 'devastating' 80 at Augusta into context.

****

While Rory was in Haiti, three other top golfers were in the White House. Davis Love, Phil Mickelson and Bubba Watson presented US president Barack Obama with a set of clubs and a new golf bag. Left-handed Obama may have even picked up a few tips from 'Lefty' Mickelson!

The trio made the presentation to the president just a few hours before he teed off in his very own open golf competition. Obama was playing in the 'Debt Limit Open', as it was dubbed by CBS White House correspondent Mark Knoller. Almost 160 golfers made it into the US Open field, but just four lined up for the Debt Limit Open: the president; his vice-president Joe Biden; Republican John Boehner, the speaker of the House of Representatives; and fellow Republican John Kasich, the governor of Ohio.

Boehner was quoted as saying: "Saturday is just about golf – and

I hope it is only about golf." He was referring, tongue-in-cheek, to the suspicion that Obama had organised the golf as a sweetener in advance of a deal to be reached in August on raising the USA's $14.3 trillion debt. Obama would require the support of Republicans for that!

The overwhelming favourite for the Debt Limit 'green jacket' was Biden. With a six handicap, *Golf Digest* has him ranked at 29 in Washington's top 150 golfers. But he would face stiff competition from Republican Boehner, an eight handicapper.

Obama took up golf as a teenager in Hawaii and is ranked 108 on the list. He remains tight-lipped on his golf game but rumour has it that he is somewhere around the 17 handicap mark. The word is that he is desperately trying to get that mark down and has been criticised in some quarters for playing too much golf. Weather permitting, he tries to get in one round of golf a week.

It is a fact that 15 of the last 18 US presidents played golf, the exceptions being Herbert Hoover, Harry Truman and Jimmy Carter. Dwight Eisenhower could not get enough of it: he had a putting green installed close to the Oval Office!

Just for the record, a White House statement gave the result of the 'DLO' as follows: "The foursome had a great time and really enjoyed playing golf at Joint Base Andrews today. The president and speaker Boehner teamed up to beat the vice-president and governor Kasich. The match was won on the 18th hole – the president and the speaker won $2 each.

"After finishing their round, the president, speaker Boehner, the vice-president and governor Kasich went to the patio of the clubhouse where they enjoyed a cold drink, some of the US Open coverage and visited with service members."

****

Rory travelled from Haiti to the golf course just ten miles from Capitol Hill in Washington where, in a few days, a major champion would be crowned. After hitting and putting a few balls in a practice round, he said on Twitter: "I saw Congressional for the first time today. I've got to draw the ball a lot so hopefully that will suit me." Earlier he had said: "I've now got all my prep work done so now I can put all my energy into Thursday – Sunday."

The US Open, as befits all majors, is a severe test with its own unique traits and trends. Britain's Open Championship has its links courses which, in tennis terms, is like playing on hard courts. Golfers also have to deal with winds sweeping in from the sea. Augusta has its lightning fast greens, which can be like ice rinks. But US Opens are notorious for being so tough that almost every golfer in the field ends up with high scores. The most notorious have been held on former Indian reservation lands.

Courses like Shinnecock Hills, Winged Foot and Oakmont are just such golf courses. When Corey Pavin won at Shinnecock in 1995, no golfer finished under par. But the winning scores on the other two courses were even worse. Scarcely believable for modern day majors, Australian Geoff Ogilvy triumphed at Winged Foot in 2006 on five over par. He had a one-shot advantage in hand over Phil Mickelson, Colin Montgomerie and Jim Furyk, who all finished at +6. At Oakmont a year later, Angel Cabrera won with a similar high score of five over. Coincidentally, Furyk once more finished in the runner-up berth – again with a score of +6.

It was no surprise that these events were highly controversial. Great golfers do not like to be humiliated. Scoring has improved in recent years but nonetheless, going into Congressional, the majority of golfers and golf pundits still expected a tough test.

Many of the top names in golf were predicting another brutally tough US Open. However, even though he had not much experience, McIlroy disagreed. Having seen the course and after getting a good feel for it, he said: "I reckon it will play a little under-par for the week. I love this set up."

Ernie Els, the US Open champion on the last occasion it was held at Congressional in 1997, spoke very highly of McIlroy at a press conference. He said: "I think he is a future world number one, without any doubt. He can really change history again. He's got that kind of talent that is going to win a lot of majors."

When told about Ernie's comments, Rory winced with embarrassment and said: "It's very flattering and it's great that people are saying I'm going to win majors, but I need to do it first. Hopefully I'll be sitting in front of the media on Sunday night saying 'yeah, maybe I could be a multiple major winner.'"

Rory began his US Open in the company of Dustin Johnson and Phil Mickelson. It was somewhat ironic that he was paired with Mickelson, for during the many weeks McIlroy took off from the tour, 'Lefty' had been very vocal and critical of Rory. Whether or not that had any bearing on Rory's mindset is irrelevant, as he birdied the first hole. The fact is, it was the perfect start and things were to get even better, to the point that Mickelson would actually end up applauding many of Rory's shots.

Rory made par at the next two holes and then birdied the 470-yard par four fourth. He also birdied the par five sixth and parred the remaining holes to be out in 33 shots, three under par. Already, it was the sort of score that would have captured many US Open titles.

On the away home, he birdied the twelfth to move to -4. After four straight pars, he then made another birdie at the par four 17th. And standing on the 18th tee, Rory took out the driver and unleashed a mighty drive down the monster 523-yard par four fairway. It was his best drive of the day and it set up his sixth birdie, with no bogeys on his card. He could afford to glance up at the scoreboard. It showed that he was out on his own at 66, six under par and three clear of Charl Schwartzel, with Sergio Garcia in third.

It was an incredible performance, in US Open terms a flawless first round. And it was the perfect way to respond after the Masters, but it was early days and there were still three more rounds to play.

The second round would prove to be one of the most momentous in Rory's career thus far. It would go on to make all sorts of headlines. So let us tag along the side of the fairway and follow every shot he made in that round.

On the 402-yard par four first hole, Rory drove his tee shot into the left semi-rough. But his approach made the green and he secured par with two putts. At the par three second, he also found the green and made par.

A superb drive down the centre of the fairway, followed by a nice iron shot to 20 feet, set up a good birdie chance on the third, a par four. But another chance went by and he had to be content with a par.

Rory's first birdie of the day eventually arrived on the fourth as a great drive was followed by an iron shot to 25 feet. He read the line of the putt perfectly as it rolled in from a left-to-right break. That birdie took him to seven under par.

McIlroy then suffered a bit of bad luck on the fifth, hitting a 3-wood right into the middle of the fairway. This left him with just a wedge to the green. But he got under the ball too much and it spun back off the green. He two-putted for another par.

The 555-yard par five sixth hole represented another chance to stretch his lead. Things did not look too good when he pulled his drive into the left rough and he was forced to lay up. But he played a magnificent shot to six feet with a wedge and duly birdied the hole.

Ominously for the rest of the field, Rory was now eight under, and he was looking hungry for more birdies. He made two putts for par on the seventh and then had the crowds and players in rapturous applause on the eighth. Philip Reid of the *Irish Times* tells us why: "McIlroy hit an iron off the tee, a short par four measuring 350 yards. With 114 yards left to the flag, he gripped down on the club and hit a half-wedge. He knew it was good. But how good?

"It pitched 30 feet past the hole and spun back, being sucked into the hole as if by some magnetic power, for an eagle two! There was no nod from Mickelson. There was a genuine grin and an actual round of applause from the four-time major winner."

At -10, Rory was now getting out of control, and the next hole was a par five with the promise of a birdie. However, he found a greenside bunker and had to settle for par. It was the first of five consecutive pars before he wove another bit of magic on the 14th, hitting another splendid drive before nailing his six-iron to just six feet. He duly sank the birdie and was now at 11 under par.

Another par followed on the 15th before another dazzling bit of play from Rory on the 16th hole drew wild roars and applause from the crowd. Playing 579 yards, he drove the ball some 350 yards to the par five and left just an iron into the green. The club he chose was a 4-iron and his shot was majestic. It stopped ten feet from the pin and he had a glorious chance to eagle and move to 13 under. He missed, but a tap-in birdie ensued and Rory was way out in front of the US Open field on -12.

At that point, he had a ten-shot lead with Brandt Snedeker, Robert Garrigus and Sergio Garcia the next in contention – on two under par. Taking Rory out of the field, the others were all playing a true and difficult US Open at 'a little under par', as Rory had predicted pre-tournament. Surely not even he could ever have imagined he would be this far out on his own, or so far under par.

Nor did it stop there. McIlroy was on fire and, at the 17th, he even had a little slice of luck to help him. After finding the middle of the fairway, he hit a 7-iron to the green but it just cleared the bunker and finished up five paces from the hole. An explosion of noise followed another birdie. Rory was -13 and all the records were falling. At that point he had broken the record for the lowest score at any point in US Open history. Tiger Woods and Gil Morgan had held the previous record at 12 under par.

Disaster struck at the final hole, however, and it brought Rory and everybody else a little way back down to earth. On that monster 523 yard par four (big enough for a par five on most other courses), which he had birdied the previous day, he could only bogey. After finding trees off the tee and water off his second shot, he was forced to take a penalty drop. He still made a great pitch to 12 feet, and then took two putts to finish out with a six and a double-bogey.

There were still plenty of reasons to smile. He must have scarcely believed his eyes when he looked at the leaderboard. At the halfway stage, with rounds of 65, 66 and leading the way at -11, he was going to take some catching. South Korean YE Yang came out of the pack to add a little respectability to the scoreboard. A 69 to add to his opening round of 68 put him on six under par, five shots adrift. Yang had famously beaten Tiger in a head-to-head for the USPGA in 2009.

Two of Rory's fellow professionals paid very generous tribute to him at the halfway stage. This is what Snedeker had to say. In any other US Open he would have been right in the mix at two under, but he had high praise for McIlroy, saying: "I think everybody would agree that Rory's got more talent in his pinky (little finger) than I have in my whole body. He is so unbelievably talented, shooting those kinds of numbers and swinging the golf club the way he does."

Snedeker added: "I love watching him play because it's a very classical, beautiful golf swing. Once he matures and starts being out here (US Tour) for a while, and being in these kinds of situations, I think he's only going to get harder to beat."

On the same score as Snedeker at -2, Garcia said: "I have bigger worries than Rory McIlroy. But he's a wonderful player and a very nice kid. I get along very well with him, too. It would be nice (if I did not win and he does) because even if what happened at Augusta did not happen, it would be nice for him to win. I think he deserves it."

Nor did Rory show any signs of fatigue. In his third round he had a steady start, making par at the first four holes. He birdied the fifth, made pars at the next three and then made another birdie at the par five ninth to take his score to -13.

It was mesmerising golf. Rory was tearing apart all the traditions of your stereotypical 'tough' US Opens, in the process, making many experienced and talented professionals look ordinary. To them, as well as to many onlookers, it must surely have seemed as if things were becoming embarrassingly easy.

Six pars, two birdies and just one bogey coming home left Rory at the top on 14 under par. After three rounds, he was eight shots ahead of Yang, with the rest floundering.

A well-worn phrase now went around; the US Open was 'his to lose'. After Augusta, however, nobody was taking anything for granted – least of all Rory.

****

To the assembled press afterwards, Rory revealed that he had gone into the third round with a plan. Furthermore, reading between the lines, he also had a plan for the final round. He was confident he knew where he had gone wrong at the Masters: "The big goal I set for myself was to try to get to 15 [under]," he said. "I didn't quite achieve it, but I don't mind. I was trying to play little three-hole stretches in one under or level par, just trying to break it down into segments instead of really getting ahead of yourself … just little triggers that make you less worried about the result and more focused on what you're actually doing."

In pursuit of a Masters green jacket, he had had a four-shot lead over the field after the third round. This time he had an even bigger lead, but he was adamant that he would not make the same mistake twice, adding: "From the experience that I had at Augusta, I now know how to approach this final round. I think that's the most important thing. At Augusta, it was all a little bit new to me – going into the final round with the lead. I didn't know whether to be defensive, aggressive, go for it or not go for it. But now I know what I need to do, which is a great thing to have. I have a clear mind going out there, and I just need to stick to my game plan."

For Rory's own sake, and for his peace of mind, he had to win from such a position. He could not afford to lose this one. If he did happen to throw it away, it could take him many years to recover – if at all.

Perhaps that's why, on this occasion, there was a rather subdued feeling enveloping Ireland. Perhaps people were keeping their fingers crossed. Perhaps they even felt that on this occasion, Rory was about to win his first major. He was so far ahead that nobody could catch him. Whatever the mood was, it was certainly nowhere near as excited as it was in the build-up to Augusta's final round.

In any case, Rory and his supporters never had a moment's worry. Because when he birdied the very first hole, not only was he home and hosed at 15 under par, but his confident and relaxed demeanour signalled to everyone that there would be no hint of failure.

One could feel the huge sigh of relief. One could see it! With his first major in the bag, Rory now opened up. Instead of relaxing and playing the percentages, he went out in a blaze of glory. He put on the style for the entire world to see. As if the first three rounds had not already been full of magical golf, Rory stamped his authority all over the tournament with some glittering golf.

Another birdie followed at the par four third. At -16, he was turning the event into a stroll in the park. Statisticians were searching for the next record to fall among the two dozen or more that had already been created.

Five pars in a row were followed by the coup de grace. At the par three tenth hole, Rory played the most beautiful iron shot. It was a shot befitting a major champion. It was also the shot that his US Open triumph will be forever remembered by.

His iron from the tee was struck with a full swing, and he loved the feel of what he had just struck. Watching the flight of the ball, he soon realised he had a hit a peach of a shot. The quality of it forced him to crouch on bended knees, willing the ball to be good. Landing 16 feet over the pin, the ball spun back slowly. It then became clear why Rory was so excited.

As the crowd rose to see the ball spinning back, the excitement mounted. The usual roars and hollers of "get in the hole" went up. This one certainly looked like it was going to obey everyone's requests. But at the very last moment it broke a little and then stopped – eight inches from the cup.

It was so close to a hole in one or, as golfing parlance now terms it, an ace. The crowd went wild as Rory approached to tap it in. The fat lady joined in and started her song. Not even a bogey at the 12th could ruin what was about to transpire. Another birdie, another bogey ensued and then Rory tapped in a tiddler for par on the 18th and final hole to win his first major.

Dad Gerry raced over from greenside and, as Rory saw him approaching, his face creased into the biggest, widest-eyed Irish smile you ever saw. At the same time he could be heard exclaiming: "Happy Father's Day!" That greeting meant more to him and Gerry than any Father's Day card, or even all of the $1.4 million dollars he had just won. To a young man with the world at his feet, and set to become a multi-millionaire, prize-money meant nothing.

The title was payback time for his family and those closest to him who had nurtured his talent over the years. He was quick to point this out. After the official presentation of the trophy, the 22-year-old said: "Happy Father's Day, Dad – this one's for you." Later he added: "I can't thank them enough."

Rory was referring to the fact that at one stage, his father Gerry had worked at three different jobs while his mother Rosie worked nights in a factory that produced miles and miles of tape. They drove and flew the young Rory to competitions all over the world. They helped with the purchase of golf gear, golf merchandise and golf lessons. The years of growing and learning certainly cost time, hard work and money invested and sacrificed. Now, all the investments and sacrifices had paid off.

****

The morning after the fantastic night before, Rory was up bright and early at his Marriott Hotel base in Bethesda. He and Gerry finally had some breathing space as they fell back into the plush settees in the hotel foyer. They both scoured the early morning editions of the day's newspapers provided for them by the reception staff. Both were wide-eyed with delight at the marvellous front-page headlines.

In particular, they admired the full-colour photographs that stood out on the front pages of America's greatest dailies. The snap they really admired was one on the front of the *Washington Post*, which showed the two of them embracing.

Their concentration was broken by a lady who came over to ask Rory to sign a T-shirt. This gave licence to a few more onlookers to approach. One held out a giant-sized US Open golf ball to be signed. Then father and son were alone again.

Another few minutes of quality time followed. Rory then turned on his mobile, saying: "I'm just checking for messages. Darren Clarke was one of the first people to call me. He rang me at 6am!"

Rory's manager, Chubby Chandler, then approached and told the young golfer and his father that their car was waiting. Outside the hotel, a people carrier was waiting to usher Rory to the airport. They were on their way to Cape Cod. There was no time for Rory to dwell on his first major win, no time to celebrate. He had made a commitment some time before to play in a private event, and he was on his way to honour that promise.

In the car, he turned to his dad and said that he had better ring a very important person straight away. Gerry gave him an approving nod and it was out with the mobile to ring his beloved Mammy. "Hi. How are you? Listen, I'm sorry I didn't ring you last night ... yes, he's here beside me ... yeah, US Open champion, it's great! OK, I'll chat to you later ... I love you too."

On the private jet to Cape Cod, Chandler and Gerry read the

papers from cover to cover. Rory curled up in a ball at the back of the plane to get some rest.

At Mashpee, Massachusetts, near the waters of Cape Cod, lies Willowbend Country Club. Here Rory signed autographs and posed for photographs with several hundred invited guests. As he did so, Gerry gave his brief thoughts on the US Open: "To be totally honest, from the age of 12 or 13, I knew he was good and so I knew he would one day do it. But I never thought it would happen so quickly. I thought maybe when he's 25 or 26."

Then, young kids with their parents and grandparents watched with open mouths as the golfer they had watched on their televisions the night before drove off from tees; played irons to greens; and putted like they had never seen before.

After eating he was off again. This time he was on his way from Cape Cod to Heathrow. In such hectic times, Rory was very grateful for one particular kind act, as he explained: "The local police chief here is an Irishman and he organised a police escort to the airport with no traffic at all, which was great. He also organised for me to go straight through without having to check in. So that's great. It beats having to queue."

Two security men standing outside the terminal building stretched out their hands to congratulate Rory. They had watched him win the Open the previous night. Rory found it all very amusing.

It was much the same at the other end, in Heathrow. As Rory waited to collect his luggage, making no effort to disguise himself, people came up to shake his hand.

Finally, at 6.30pm, he flew into George Best International Airport – in pouring rain. On the descent to the runway, he glanced out of the window and started pointing out places that he was familiar with. He was glad to be home, and two very special ladies were awaiting his arrival.

When he walked through the front door of his plush home on the outskirts of Holywood, his mother Rosie embraced him with a huge hug and kiss. Rory presented her with the magnificent silver US Open trophy. Later he said: "That hug from my mum is something I'll never forget. It was so special and it meant so much."

Down the stairs came Rory's girlfriend, Holly Sweeney. Another big hug and kiss and then they went over to sift through and read letters and emails from eminent people. Later, Rory went out for a Chinese meal with his family.

Before that, and as he relaxed in his home catching up on all that had gone on with his parents and Holly, Rory did something rather amusing. Taking a snap of the US Open trophy, he placed it on Twitter along with the message: "Great to be back home. Even nicer to have this on my kitchen table … and for anyone who's interested, there will be no open-top bus parade through Belfast! I'm a golfer, not a football team!"

The next day, Rory travelled to Holywood Golf Club, where it had all begun for him. At the entrance to the town of Holywood, a big roadside banner of congratulation caught his attention. From the passenger window of the car, he snapped the image on his mobile.

At the golf club, he stood out on a balcony holding the recently won trophy. Speaking to all of his fellow club golfers and friends just below him, he said: "I'm so proud to be from here. I've won this US Open trophy but I'd just like you to know that it belongs to all of you."

Among many visits and presentations, perhaps one of his last put his achievement into another, deeper perspective. After a rip-roaring return to his former school, Sullivan Upper, with all the pupils shaking his hand and taking photographs, he quipped: "I didn't think a few years ago that I would be back here and experiencing that – teachers coming up to me and asking for autographs!"

Chapter 3:
An Open Sandwich

Following his US Open triumph there was huge excitement and anticipation ahead of Rory's appearance just a few weeks later at the Open Championship at Royal St George's. There were many who were now touting him as a back-to-back major winner.

Not since Phil Mickelson and Tiger Woods (remember him?) had there been such a short-priced favourite for a major. Bookmakers actually put Rory up as 6/1 favourite. Rorymania was breaking out everywhere. Sponsors wanted a piece of him; media requested interviews with him; photographers were looking for his next social outing; and the public were beginning to adore him. Suddenly, Rory McIlroy was the biggest sports star and the number one golfer on the planet.

The boy had come along way in a short space of time. His tag of Open favourite was due in part to his stunning first round at St Andrews the previous year. But he had made his mark and left an impression on the Open even before that.

When he made his debut at Carnoustie in 2007 as an amateur, McIlroy was a general 1,000/1 chance with the layers. But that did not stop one writer spotting his talents and singing it from the rooftops.

The *Racing Post's* chief golf writer and tipster Jeremy Chapman, under a banner headline entitled: 'McIlroy the boy who will one day become king', prophetically wrote: "There is the chance this week to be in at the start of something special and also profit from it. Bookmakers are going 5/2 that Rory McIlroy finishes top of the six competing amateurs.

"A slightly built 18-year-old from Holywood, Northern Ireland, he is the European Amateur Champion and he will turn pro after the Walker Cup in September. He has already shot 61 at Royal Portrush, the links that hosted the 1951 Open.

"He hits the ball 300 yards; has already played three times on the European Tour; counts Darren Clarke among his fan club; and he should finish top amateur this weekend.

"Richie Ramsay, who just failed to make the cut at Augusta, is the favourite and will be a tough nut to crack. He will have the full weight of Scottish support behind him, but it is McIlroy who will one day be the superstar."

On Thursday, 19 July 2007, at 1.42pm, Rory McIlroy made his Open debut, teeing off in the company of Spanish legend Miguel Angel Jimenez and Sweden's Henrik Stenson. Rory would justify Chapman's hopes in him as well as serve notice to the golf world of his arrival on the major stage. When he finished his round and looked up at the scoreboard, only two of the 160-odd players had bettered his score.

Sergio Garcia shot the best of the day, 65 to lead on six under par, while Ireland's Paul McGinley was two shots back on 67. Rory fired a three under par 68. Richie Ramsay shot 76 and, with a 75 in the next round, he missed the cut. Chapman's tip romped to victory.

The next day was not so good. McIlroy came home in 76 but further improvement with his final rounds of 73 and 72 meant he was the leading amateur. He took home the prize of the silver salver and finished tied 42nd overall. As he stood at the presentation ceremony beside winner Padraig Harrington, the speeches and acknowledgements went on and on. Perhaps it allowed Rory the time to daydream that he too might one day lift the famous claret jug.

Harrington made it back-to-back Opens by winning again the following year, but Rory did not make it to Royal Birkdale. In 2009, he did not play well and finished tied 47th. However, he was back with a vengeance at the home of golf in 2010.

St Andrews is not only one of the Open's flagship golf courses, it is also one of the most famous golf courses in the world – perhaps *the* most famous. With its notorious Road Hole bunker, as well as the unique 17th and 18th holes, it has a mind of its own. When the day is calm, it can be a beautiful course yielding low scores. But when the wind and rain blow in, it can be a dreadful test for everyone. Perhaps that is why it is often referred to as a lady.

Rory McIlroy loves the place. He has never had a bad experience there, as an amateur or as a professional. And when he teed off in the first round, he was embarking upon another very special and record-breaking journey.

McIlroy birdied the third to go into red figures and, after making par at every hole from the fourth to the eighth, he shot a magnificent eagle at the par four ninth to go to three under. Then he took off like a man possessed, and there was no stopping him.

He birdied three more holes in a row from the tenth to the 12th to go to -7, and he did not stop there. After making it six beautiful birdies in seven holes at the 15th, he sent the spectators wild with delight by finishing off on the 18th with yet another birdie.

Rory had torn the course apart. Seven birdies, an eagle and no dropped shots meant he was all alone at the top on nine under par. It was an astonishing round. Afterwards he was gracious when he said: "Going out there this morning with no wind, you're never going to get St Andrews playing any easier."

His 63 tied for the lowest score in any major, and it was only the second such score at St Andrews in golf's oldest championship. McIlroy was also the youngest player to shoot 63 in a major – just 21 years and 72 days old. Of the eight players who have shot 63 in Open history, McIlroy had also become the first, and so far, only one to do it in the first round.

Some of his shots were simply breathtaking, out of this world. For instance, his amazing run really kicked off with a drive that ran up on to the green at the 352-yard ninth hole to about 15 feet below the hole. He knocked that in for an eagle, and there's no doubt it inspired him.

The freckle-faced Holywood boy then followed that with a sand wedge to six feet on the tenth for birdie; a 7-iron to eight feet for birdie on the 11th, and two putts from 50 feet on the short 12th hole for that fourth birdie in a row.

More followed at 14, 15 and 18, but the greedy part of our human nature is such that we still always talk about the one that got away. Rory had a glorious chance to rewrite the record books outright in his own name.

When he was eight under par, he flew his approach dangerously close over the Road Hole bunker on the 17th, leaving him a five-foot birdie putt. Unbelievably, after what he had done in his previous holes, he missed! It almost certainly cost him a 62 and he revealed afterwards: "It sort of went through my mind on 17 that 62 would have been the lowest round in a major. That's probably why I missed the putt."

To be fair, there were 44 other scores in the 60s on that opening day. Even when the wind got up after Rory finished his round, four players shot 66, prompting Tom Watson to quip: "The old lady had no clothes on today!"

Rory had played nine rounds at St Andrews in his young career, and had finished every one of them under 70. But the second round was to be an entirely different kettle of fish. The old lady wrapped up well and Rory was in for a shock.

He made par at the first three holes to remain -9 and then he made his first bogey in 22 holes at the fifth. However, worse was to follow. Incredibly, he bogeyed three in a row from holes six to eight, to fall from -9 to -5. He was shell-shocked.

Ashen faced, Rory was not to be spared. Whatever he had taken in the previous round, he was now being forced to give it back. A double-bogey followed at 11 and with further bogeys at 13 and 15, his day had turned into a real nightmare. Eight shots dropped and not a single birdie all day was the cruellest of blows. How could she have become such a vile and pernicious woman? From being in a strong position to have a shot at winning the Open at -9, only to plummet down to -1, must have been nauseating.

There were mitigating circumstance in the strong winds, and the players were even called off the course for a time. However, Rory refused to use any excuses and he said he could have hit 82 or 83 as he was lucky to par the last three holes.

From ecstasy to agony and from 63 to 80, it seemed as if Rory had gone from full pelt to wilting sails. As is his nature however, he fought back. The words 'sulk', 'submit' and 'surrender' are not in Rory McIlroy's dictionary.

After that second round he said: "It all depends what the weather is like. If it's calm, I feel as if I've got a chance to go make a few birdies again and go low. And if the wind is like this again, you're relying on the leaders to sort of mess up a little bit because it's very hard to make up ground when the wind is this strong."

For Rory, the only way forward – the only way he knows – is a constant quest for the sublime. OK, so he had a bogey and double-bogey on his card again the next day. But he offset that with six birdies to climb back up the leaderboard, finishing on four under par.

A neat and tidy front nine on the last day saw Rory rise to -6, with birdies on the fifth and ninth. A bogey followed on the 11th but it was to be his last. He finished with three more fantastic birdies for a four round total of 280 – eight under par.

That score was never going to be good enough to trouble runaway winner Louis Oosthuizen and the South African won his first major by seven shots from Lee Westwood. Rory could be proud of his efforts though, and he finished tied third.

As John Giles might say, "there's no such thing as 'ifs', 'buts' and 'maybes'". You can add to that 'only for' and then come to the realisation that Rory would have been in the mix with Oosthuizen if it hadn't been for that fateful second round. So it was easy to see why the public, en masse, expected him to triumph again. With his class, resilience and courage on links courses, the boy had the potential to be crowned a British king. Royal St George's, Sandwich now beckoned.

****

Rory's preparations for the 2011 Open began by getting in some practice at the course. But a week before the event, and just a day before getting that important feel of the Royal St George's course,

Tiger Woods pulled out of the Open. It was no big surprise. In fact, it was expected as Tiger decided to take a little longer to return to competitive golf from injury.

On his way to Kent, Rory also brought something over with him – a long lost friend he had found. Chubby Chandler explained: "He's got a new Titleist driving iron in the bag for next week. I think he found it lying around the garage. He's excited about it as he reckons he can get it out there at around 260 yards. He can hit it low and it's very strong in the wind."

McIlroy revealed he was delighted to find the club as he hadn't used it in six years and it was a very handy weapon to use in windy conditions. The wind at St Andrew's that contributed to his 80 in 2010 helped his decision to take the club. "He's been working on his wind game for a while and he can hit the ball any height he wants. I don't foresee any problems. Rory can hit the ball two feet off the ground if he wants to," his coach Michael Bannon revealed.

A funny thing happened in his practice round. Rory, who loves dogs and has two of his own, was followed around the course by a black Labrador. The media had a field day when they learned the dog's name – Midas! Would Rory find a golden touch?

He returned home to Holywood for a weekend of relaxation and then, on the Monday before the Open, spent some quality time with Gerry. It sometimes seemed as if all the travelling and other commitments left no time for the family, as Rory said: "My mum and dad have been just as busy so it was great to get a little bit of time together. Just myself and my dad playing a round and having a good chat. It brought back a lot of memories of playing with Dad on long summer nights, teeing off at 7pm and getting back in a few hours later. It also gives you time to get things settled in your head."

Off the course, things started off with a bit of a hiccup for McIlroy the day before the event: he was stranded for almost two hours at Manston Airport in Kent when his courtesy car failed to arrive. The private jet carrying him from Belfast touched down at 10am but the Open organisers had arranged for a car to pick him up at noon. Rory could only hope that this was not a bad omen ahead of his 9.10am tee-off time next day.

So what about Royal St George's – better known as Sandwich – the Open course he was about to play? Let the *Racing Post's* Jeremy Chapman give you an insight into it through this hilarious piece about a round he played there: "On the stark Kent course at Sandwich, just a few miles north of Dover, they are a strange breed. They dress from another century, another time, collars and ties are everywhere – don't dare go in some of the clubhouse rooms without them – and women golfers don't even have their own tees.

"The fair sex are just about permitted on the course but have to play from the men's markers and if any male gathering wants to play through them, the ladies are treated as if they are transparent.

"I've covered four Opens there and I even saw the legendary Arnold Palmer win his final proper tournament there in his 46th year when he won the 1975 Colgate PGA title.

"Until April 2011, I'd never played the ancient links that hosted the first Open on English terrain in 1894 and the first of Harry Vardon's victories in 1904. I'd never actually wanted to play there either because none of the holes looked remotely attractive. It was how I imagined playing golf on the moon might be.

"But finally I made it, aged 69, to the Royal & Ancient media day and I began better than Tiger Woods did on his St George's debut in 2003. Well, at least I didn't lose the ball with my opening tee shot like he did.

"If they had found Tiger's ball in time, he would have been in a playoff with the eventual winner, Ben Curtis. That ball, a Nike, was newly launched in the UK that week. It was later found by a volunteer marshal who sold it to the *Sun* newspaper.

"At least Tiger and I have one thing in common. I scored the same as him at number one – an inglorious seven. The good news is that seven was to be my worst score of the day. The bad news is that there were nine of them. Sadly, Tiger's score would eventually beat mine by 34 shots over the following 17 holes.

"My one and only par came at the Maiden. Ian Fleming called it the Virgin in his novel *Goldfinger*. Both names were presumably inspired by early photographs depicting twin sandy mounds. Apparently, one player chalked up a 45 there. I had a three. It should have been a two but it was a fluke anyway. I pushed my 9-wood tee shot towards a mound on my right. I was looking for it there in the rough or in one of the bunkers close by when I heard one of my partners shout: 'Whose ball is that next to the flag?'

"Would you believe it was my ball? I mean, it threaded its way through two mounds and three bunkers and it was nestling just four feet from the hole. Naturally, I was so gob-smacked that the birdie putt never even touched the sides.

"As the closest to the pin on the day at number six, it was still worth a bottle of the R&A's finest Scotch whisky. I needed every drop of it as I counted up my score at the end of my 270 minutes in the torture chamber. A good score if your name was Smith or Strauss but not so hot from a Mickelson or Westwood."

On the first tee, Rory looked nervous. There seemed to be a bit of tension in his shoulders. All the days and weeks of intense reporting, questioning and speculation gave one the impression that he wished he was not the centre of a media frenzy.

Then he broke into a smile when he spotted Ricky Fowler and chatted with the American. They had played the first two rounds at the US Masters and enjoyed good banter there, so it looked like Rory was now relaxed among friends he knew.

Although he was the only one of the three-ball to have a 2-iron in his bag, he settled down to drive his ball off with a 3-wood. He gave it a confident strike and his first shot of the 2011 Open went down the right. It was a perfect start.

Walking down the first fairway from the tee, Rory chatted with his other playing partner, South African legend Ernie Els. It was a striking sight: Rory looked like a mere boy in comparison to Els, who towered over him.

All three played their shots on to the green with McIlroy and Fowler facing long putts from the very back. The smile broke across Rory's face again a few minutes later as Fowler holed his monster 60-foot putt for birdie.

Rory had the perfect line on it. His ball was just to the right of Fowler's and it was a little closer. In reading it, he would now know that the putt swung (broke) viciously from right to left as he looked at it and the swing would start five feet from the hole. But the smile turned to a grimace as he read it totally wrong. This was a cardinal sin from someone of Rory's class. He actually went left and the ball ended up six feet from the hole. He now had a tricky putt for par, which he missed. It was a bad start.

One over par after one hole, Rory then found the semi-rough to the right of the tee. He recovered with a beautiful iron approach into the centre of the green, leaving him 30 feet for birdie. He left it short but holed for par. The BBC's Ken Brown said: "He was too strong on the green at the first and too weak on the second. He is trying to find his touch."

At the third, the BBC's on-course reporter, Maureen Madill, commented: "I think Ernie Els is getting a real buzz out of playing with these youngsters. Ernie actually turned professional the year Rory was born!" But Rory was getting no such buzz, as things were about to get worse. His 4-iron shot went straight through to the back of the green. He fluffed his chip coming back, leaving him with yet another dangerous par putt. He missed and he was now two over par after three holes.

He steadied the ship to the point where he put himself into beautiful positions with three good chances for birdie on the next four holes. But he did not convert any of the opportunities and things were becoming frustrating.

Then, on the eighth hole, he took out his old friend. Remember that fellow who had been tucked away in his garage for six years? Well, Rory took Mr Driving Iron out and played a shot 282 yards down the centre. He then played another iron to seven feet. Finally, he sank a birdie.

He was now back to +1 and maybe things were about to change for the better. From the ninth to the 12th, he again put himself into good position for birdies with some great iron play, but his putter was still not working well.

While McIlroy was struggling, Thomas Bjorn of Denmark was making a very difficult course look ridiculously easy and moving to five under. Bjorn had only got into the Open on the Monday as first reserve, when Vijay Singh pulled out. Incidentally, at 1.30pm, Belgian player Nicolas Colsaerts withdrew. He had fallen off a scooter earlier in the week and his injuries had not healed, allowing Ricky Barnes in as second reserve. Ricky flew over from America just in case, and his gamble paid off.

The hot favourite for the Open, Rory was now six shots behind the leader. He had six holes left to play in his round and he needed something to happen quickly for him. But it was to become even more of an uphill struggle.

On the 13th, he pulled his drive badly off the tee and ended up in deep rough. He played a great shot from the rough but was a club short. His putt had a huge swing from right to left and agonisingly, it stayed out on the lip. Another bogey and he was back to +2.

When it's not your day, things tend to go from bad to worse. On the par five 14th, Rory drove a perfect shot straight down the middle. He connected beautifully with his 3-wood second from the fairway and then winced as he watched his ball in flight. It turned in mid-air and flirted with the bunkers before catching the furthest trap from the green. Even worse, when Rory got up to close to take a look, he found the ball tucked right in under the lip.

An awkward shot, from a difficult stance, followed. Standing in the bunker on his left leg, Rory had to kneel outside the bunker on his right leg. In the circumstances, he did well just to hack his ball out on to the green, leaving him 60 feet for birdie. He putted up the green to five feet and once more a tricky putt beckoned for par. He got it.

The 15th turned into 'crazy golf', akin to something one would see in a comedy film. The difference was this was deadly serious and far from funny.

Driving off the tee, Rory watched his ball in the air anxiously – he did not like where it was going. It managed to skip past hungry bunkers but ended up in the semi-rough. After being chopped out of the rough, the ball scuttled through the green, down the undulations and finished at the back of the green. Rory was faced with a very difficult shot and another bogey looked likely.

In times of duress such as these, we so often see moments of brilliance. Rory played a real gem of a shot – a sort of semi-Mickelson Flop to just a couple of feet – to save the hole with a par.

The hard day continued, forcing him to play another masterly shot on the short par three 16th. He used the wind to help carry his ball from right to left and it finished just 20 feet from the pin. It resulted in another par and Rory remained +2 with two holes remaining.

He showed more McIlroy genius on the 17th. A monster hit saw his ball come up short in front of the bunker guarding the approach to the green. He played a gentle wedge shot but this time he used the bank at the side of the green to his advantage. The ball moved up the bank a little and then trickled back to just seven feet for birdie.

On the final hole, he played two more exquisite shots to give himself a good chance for birdie from 16 feet. But he just missed out and had to be content with a round of 71, finishing one over par.

There is a thin line between everything, as the saying goes, and it was very much a case of what might have been for Rory. He had let several frustrating chances for birdie slide past and had made too many unforced errors. But he lived to fight another day, saying: "It was OK. It was a tough day. I had to stay patient and I did make a few nice putts coming home so I'm reasonably happy."

Do tough conditions suit you, he was asked. "The harder it is, the better it will be. If I can keep it around level, I think the winner will come from around there. Par, out here, is a very good score."

On the first tee for the second round, Rory looked much happier and more relaxed than he had the previous day. He was smiling, laughing and shaking hands with everyone he laid eyes on.

His drive found the right rough but he played a magnificent second shot to within eight feet of the hole, but once again he misread the putt. He must have expected a right-to-left break. He hit it on that side but it stayed right, resulting in a tap-in for par.

After Rory missed another glorious birdie chance on the second, he was grateful to make a brilliant par-saving putt on the third. His wedge came up short of the green and was down in a dip. He misjudged his first putt and was forced to save par from 12 feet.

Another par followed but frustration was now very much the name of his game and on the fifth he missed a gilt-edged chance to get back to level par. This was a hole that Dustin Johnson had driven just a few minutes earlier. At 419 yards, he had putted for eagle. Rory almost drove it too, but his ball came up just short in the fringe at the front of the green. Nevertheless, he was only 40 feet from the hole for an eagle chance. After showing a lovely deft touch with his chip, his ball inched its way to six feet for birdie.

Yet another miss and he even managed to send it four feet past the hole! Between his opening round and his round after five holes here, Rory had had enough chances to be sharing the lead, or better, with Bjorn at -5. As it was, he was still one over and he desperately needed something to happen or his 2011 Open would pass him by. Inside he must have been feeling it. The agony of missing so many easy chances saps confidence and willpower.

It finally happened for Rory on the sixth. He played a dream shot, the sort of shot a golfer often pictures in his mind, but it actually happens far too rarely: in the air, down, sit stone-dead at ten to 12 feet for birdie. He nailed the putt.

Rory was now level par. The crowd hollered. There was a smile on his face and a spring in his step. Now it was full steam ahead. Kick on and make inroads into the lead. Next stop is under par.

And it happened. Frustration, agony and despair one minute; exhilaration, expectation and hope the next. A good drive on the par five seventh was followed by a long iron to the front of the green. Two putts for birdie. Yes! Rory was now one under par for the championship.

This was why he had been the Open favourite. The cream was rising to the top. From being six shots back and looking like he could even miss the cut, he was now perfectly poised with plenty of time and a long way to go.

If only it all worked out like that. The crowd expected; the viewers expected; Rory expected; but by the end of his round, he was almost back to where he started. Two bogeys, a birdie and a great par meant he finished one under for the day, level at halfway.

While Rory was experiencing two up-and-down rounds with the common denominator of frustration, the three other Irish players taking part endured contrasting fortunes. McIlroy's great friend and fellow Tweeter Graeme McDowell surprisingly missed the cut. That came at +3 with McDowell finishing +4. Dual Open champion

Padraig Harrington also missed the cut, finishing at +5.

But Darren Clarke was sitting proudly on top of the leaderboard with American Lucas Glover on -4. The man from Dungannon shot two consecutive rounds of two under par 68, but that was no surprise to Rory who, after his round, told the BBC: "He's (Darren) grown up on links and he likes to play different shots. It's the sort of week where you have to rearrange your game very well. He's good at doing that – hitting different shots and changing the trajectory. He's doing a bit better than me at the moment but I plan on changing that."

Rory added: "It was a grind today. Even though it was sunny and it looked nice out there, it was very tricky. The course is playing a lot firmer with crosswinds, and so to shoot in the 60s today means I'm very happy. It would have been nice to be a couple better but I'll take that going into the weekend. I'm very happy to be within striking distance of the leaders."

On the third day, the miserable conditions that had been forecast duly arrived. And Rory was paired with … Ricky Fowler! It was the fifth time they had been paired together in their last 12 rounds in the majors.

Fowler was wearing giant black gloves that looked like over-sized oven gloves. In fact, it seemed as if everyone on the golf course was wearing them, so some tradesman was doing great business. Actually, Phil Mickelson was wearing them with another pair of smaller gloves underneath – and he even made a five foot par putt with both sets of gloves on. Rory was dressed in all-black waterproofs.

In the circumstances, it was not surprising that Rory got off to a disastrous start. He had to make two difficult par putts in the opening three holes, and he failed. He had now slipped back to +2. On holes four and five the same old story resurfaced; he missed two glorious birdie chances.

When he came in after posting a huge score, England's Paul Casey gave viewers a taste of what it was like for himself – as well as the guys out on the course –when he said: "The problem is that there is so much water coming between the ball and the club face that it is very difficult to judge what will actually happen next."

Although Fowler was creating some fireworks and coping brilliantly with the weather, nothing else really happened for Rory until the par five 14th hole. It was to be a turning point and the defining moment at Sandwich for him.

McIlroy knew that with just a few holes left, and time running out on his British Open challenge, he had to make a birdie and perhaps even an eagle to start one more charge at the leaders. Out with the driver. Rory smashed it and then a few seconds later dropped his club and head in resignation. The ball swung to the right, behind white stakes and into fencing.

It was more than a difficult second shot. There was no second shot. In golfing lingo, his ball had just gone OOB – out of bounds. It was the end for Rory. In the circumstances, he did well to come out of it with a double-bogey seven and walk off the green at four over par.

Just under an hour later, Rory shook hands with Fowler on the 18th. He had made par on the final four holes to finish 74, +4 for the tournament. He pulled his peaked cap right down over his eyes. With that body language, he signalled that his Open was shut. He had been blown off course.

Ireland's Sunday sports supplement *The Title* ran a headline: 'McIlroy chokes on a soggy Sandwich', but that eye-catching header was perhaps a little unfair. There is no way Rory had choked or bottled his Open week. It was probably closer to the mark and a lot fairer to state what Rory later acknowledged – that he was unlucky to be drawn out in the worst of conditions. Those who did well were blessed with the best of weather.

In the final round, Rory had to watch again as a second successive playing partner tore the course asunder. Sergio Garcia was a man on fire. He went from four over to two under with an incredible six under par score through ten holes. Rory watched in disbelief, at the same time admiring and applauding the Spaniard's shots.

The wheels eventually fell off for the Spaniard, as they had for Rory a long time before. He was just going through the motions and there is little doubt the pair talked about Rory's tennis idol and great friend Rafa Nadal through the closing holes.

While it may have been disappointment for him, it was sheer joy and delight for a fellow Northern Ireland golfer. Darren Clarke romped to victory and won his first major with Rory witnessing and toasting his success.

It was the end of a frustrating week and one from which Rory could take away painful lessons – and perhaps learn from them. On the whole, though, he had shown the world enough to suggest he will become an Open champion one day.

Chapter 4:
An Amazing Amateur

When young Rory McIlroy started school at St Patrick's Primary School in Holywood, his love for golf deepened. His teacher, Maighread McCullough – or Miss McCullough to Rory – recalled how golf-mad he was: "He was cute, loveable and generally a good child. He worked very hard and he was an inspiration to the other boys in the class. But you could tell that he was very much into golf as well.

"I remember in the summer time he was on the golf course before he came to school and then he went golfing after school. He always had golf balls and tees in his pockets."

The school's principal, Geraldine Teer, acknowledged that Rory had a very special gift and talent far removed from studies. "Many of the teachers here taught Rory," she said. "When he was in fourth class he won the World Under-10s in golf, so all of us – teachers and pupils – are very proud of him. Because of that success, we had already recognised his talent from a very young age."

A Tweet for Rory on 'TheFirstTee' website after his US Open win read something like this: "Congrats on your major win – the first being the Doral Junior Publix U-10!" In 1998, when Rory was only nine years old, he won the Doral Junior Under-10 event in Miami, Florida. In various age categories, the Doral Tournament accommodates an entry list of well over 600 juniors, from all over the world. In his Under-10 category, which had an entry list of around 80, Rory ended up the victor. In fact, he did not just win – he trounced the other kids, winning by five shots. It was indeed his first 'major' win!

The boy he beat was an American from Utah named Scott Pinckney, two months older than Rory. The two struck up an immediate rapport and have remained friends ever since, as the good-humoured American explained: "My family went to Doral and Rory's family went. We met and we just hit it off. Everyone had a great time. His family wanted him to come over and play golf in the States and we developed such a relationship there that they shipped him over."

They got on so well that McIlroy stayed with the Pinckney family for three months at their home in Orem, Utah and played junior golf with his new friend. Pinckney holds dear the memories of those days: "He spent the whole summer with us and we had an awesome time. Ever since then, we have had a great relationship."

Pinckney, who is studying at Arizona State University, has always been impressed by the quality of McIlroy's ball-striking as well as his relaxed approach out on the course: "He has such a great attitude and he just oozes confidence. It's awesome to see."

But he is not just saying that from the memory of bygone days together. So firm is the lasting friendship between the two that they practised together on the eve of the 2011 US Open. Pinckney had good reason to be there, as he himself qualified for the Congressional tournament. "If he had acted any different from the Masters, it would have just hurt him," he said. "He acted perfectly. That's the sort of guy he is. He just draws from experience, good or bad, and then he builds on it."

The Doral Junior event is an obvious nursery for future talent. Pinckney was good enough to qualify for a major, but players like Chris Couch and several times US Tour winner Sean O'Hair have also won the event.

But Doral was just the start of a long line of successful events for Rory – even back then as a young boy. That same year, 1998, he won the Moyola Celebrity Golf Classic, held on the 130-acre wooded Shanemullagh Estate outside Magherafelt in County Derry. He was also third in the Junior World Championships and, to round off what had been a fantastic year, he won the coveted *Belfast Telegraph* Golfer of the Year award.

In 1999, Rory again finished third in the Junior World Championships. The event, held each year in San Diego, California caters for boys and girls in age categories from six up to 15-17 years old. For the younger kids, the competitions are held on a par three course but for the 15-17 age group, the play takes place on the US Open venue of Torrey Pines.

Like the Doral Junior Publix event, it has proved a great grounding for future stars. An impressive list of past champions at the World Juniors includes Tiger Woods, Ernie Els, Phil Mickelson, David Toms, Corey Pavin, Nick Price, Notah Begay and Craig Stadler. The year of 1984, for example, turned out to be a vintage year. Toms won the 15–17 title, Els took the 13–14s (with Mickelson finishing second) and Tiger won the 9–10s (despite being just eight years old).

It can be argued that although Rory did not add his name to an illustrious hall of fame for that event, his consistency in finishing third two years in a row, in such a huge tournament, made him a virtual honorary winner.

He also competed twice in the Pepsi Little People's Golf Championships, finishing third in 1999. Inaugurated in 1974, this is one of the largest events of its kind in the world. Open Championship winners Ben Curtis and Todd Hamilton began their careers there and one of the most unusual aspects of the event is that it is held in the small Mississippi city of Quincy – with the nearest airport 120 miles away.

Back on the other side of the pond, Rory was beginning to make a huge name for himself. In 2002, at the age of 13, he won the Ulster Boys Under-15 championship at Shandon Park. But it was the following year that he really started to get noticed.

In the Ulster Boys Open Championship at Donaghdee, he enjoyed a thrilling 19th hole victory over pre-tournament favourite Nicky Grant from Clandeboye, and he went on to contest the final. Playing in front of huge galleries, the 14-year-old McIlroy, who was by now playing off scratch, had the crowds gasping and applauding in astonishment as he hit several drives over 300 yards. In an equally splendid final, he beat County Cork lad David Daly by 3&1. Daly represented the Muskerry Golf Club, which is remarkably similar to Rory's own club of Holywood in everything from the clubhouse to the hilly course.

Quite aside from his monster drives and excellent all-round play in that final, Rory set a new record that day. In beating Daly, who now teaches golf in the US, he became the youngest winner of the Ulster Boys in 55 years.

Ireland had now woken up to a potential new golfing whizz-kid. The sky was the limit for what the curly haired youngster could achieve, especially as he was now being tipped to become even better than another Ulster prodigy, Ronan Rafferty.

Rory, aged just 15, tried to obtain his European Professional Tour card in 2004 but it was probably no surprise when, being so young, he failed to make the grade. Once again, however, it showed his lofty ambitions and above all his belief.

That same year he was selected for the GB & Ireland Junior Ryder Cup team, to play the United States in Detroit in September. It was the perfect tonic for him going into the Ulster Boys Amateur Open Championship, which he was bidding to retain.

McIlroy was in stupendous form. Playing for Ireland in the European Team Boys championship in Poland, he had come home with the distinction of having won all of his single matches. So on the strength of his rising star, it was no surprise that he was selected for that Junior Ryder Cup team. But there was one aspect of his selection that particularly pleased him. On hearing of his selection he said: "I am thrilled at the honour, especially as I'm the lone Irish player in the team."

The Junior Ryder Cup event was a new idea that gave the kids lucky enough to be selected the chance to compete in a curtain raiser to the main Ryder Cup matches. Rory helped Europe to victory.

It was no surprise in the circumstances, therefore, that Rory went on to retain his Ulster Boys Amateur Open title. But he did so by playing some of the most brilliant and majestic golf of his fledgling career. There was simply no stopping him as he went from strength to strength. Mind you, it helped somewhat that he was playing in his own backyard of Holywood – a course he knew like the back of his hand. It showed.

In the semi-final, he saw off Belvoir Park's Patrick MacMahon with relative ease, beating him 4&3 on the 15th green. Liam Reilly of Galgorm Castle was to face Rory in the final, but he exceeded all expectations by getting there. In those circumstances, and with Rory playing so well and at home, Reilly was a huge outsider with Rory the hottest of hot favourites.

Again, McIlroy never had a moment's bother. Readily brushing aside his challenger, he triumphed even more easily than in the semi-final, winning 5&4. But after retaining his title, and clearly showing that he was looking to the next step up, afterwards he had only one thing on his mind as he stated: "That's a great boost for Portmarnock next week, when I'll be representing Ireland in the Boys Home Team Championships."

With Northern Ireland well and truly conquered, Rory now set his sights on the Republic of Ireland.

****

In August 2004, Rory McIlroy won the Nissan Irish Boys Championship at Castlebar Golf Club in County Mayo. To this day, he still holds the course record: he shot a 66 on the par 72 course. Mick Byrne, a past captain at Castlebar, remembers it: "You know, even back then, Rory McIlroy was a huge name. Only 15 years old, he was still the big up-and-coming star and we all went out on the course to see him play. He had an even bigger mass of black curly hair as well!

"But to the end of my days, I'll never forget a shot he played. It was the greatest shot I ever saw played right in front of me in my entire life and I'll probably never see a greater shot.

"From his drive, off the members' white tee area, he left himself around 241 yards to the pin. I saw him take out a 3-iron and he struck it perfectly on to the green, where he eagled it!"

Michael Ryan, the club professional at Oughterard in County Galway, recalls a similar event. Rory broke the course record there in August 2003 playing in the Connacht Boys Championship. Playing off scratch, the 14-year-old posted a front nine score of 35 and a back nine of 32, for a 67. The record was beaten in 2005 by Eoin O'Connor, who shot 65, but Ryan remembers the day, if not the play, that Rory tore up the course. "I was busy in the club shop but I saw him on the first tee and later on the 12th when I was driving through the village. You can remember those little things because people were all talking about him even then, and he had a certain aura about him."

Even outside golf, the awards were now beginning to fall at Rory's feet. After winning the Junior Sports Star of the Year title in Ireland at the end of 2004, another award came his way just before the 2005 West Of Ireland Championships. As he began his preparations for one of Ireland's most prestigious amateur golf titles, to be held at Rosses Point in County Sligo, he was presented with the *Irish Examiner* Junior Golfer of the Year award.

Around this time, Rory decided to leave school. He had not been happy studying for some time, for he just wanted to play golf for a career. He knew he could make it as a professional; his father knew it; and his advisors knew it. It was just a matter of time. So, before his GCSEs, McIlroy went into Sullivan Upper School in Holywood to see his superiors. By the time he came out of the principal's office, he was free to walk the fairways of the world. And his first excursion was a case of 'Go West Young Man'.

Travelling to the west of Ireland for a few days of intense competition, Rory had done his homework with father Gerry and coach Michael Bannon. He knew he was going to face very stiff competition from Scandanavia.

Sweden had a very strong representation with no fewer than ten golfers, including the top-rated man for the event in Rikard Karlberg. Indeed, Mikko Illonen of Finland had won this event when it was held at Enniscrone, Sligo in 1999. However, two home-based players fought out a very memorable final. Mallow's David Finn really put it up to Rory, who eventually won 2&1. He had just become the youngest ever winner of the West of Ireland championship.

On the Slugger O'Toole website, Mick Fealty wrote: "Congratulations to Holywood boy Rory McIlroy on winning the West Of Ireland Golf Championship at Rosses Point in Sligo, at the grand old age of 15.

"Last time I saw him, he'd just flown back from Florida with his dad where they'd been readying a course in preparation for the World Under-10s Championship (back in 98, I think) in time to grab a bite to eat and up and out on to the Holywood course. At the time, as I recall, his golf bag was slightly longer than he was tall. It seems he's grown, in stature as well as in years!"

Following his West of Ireland triumph, Rory was selected by the Golfing Union of Ireland to compete in the Nissan Irish Open Championship. That year it was played over the Montgomerie course at Carton House Golf Club on May 19.

But the Irish Open was not actually Rory's debut on the European Tour. Three months earlier, on February 5, he had played as an amateur in the Dubai Desert Classic, the cut with rounds of 72 and 72.

His upward curve continued when he went on to add the Irish Close Championship to his West of Ireland. Again, he became the youngest ever winner of that event, being six months younger than a certain Ronan Rafferty had been when he won the tournament in 1981.

Sixteen-year-old McIlroy played 32-year-old Eddie McCormack, nowadays a sales representative for Gleeson Wines, in the final at Westport. Still trudging the amateur fairways of Ireland and Europe, the affable and bubbly Galwegian looks back on that day with a lot of good memories: "You know, I was actually playing shite going into the Irish Close and I wasn't happy with my form at all," he recalled. "But when the competition started, I was a totally different animal and I enjoyed a thrilling semi-final win in the morning."

Eddie says that because he was 'in the zone' and all his form came together for that Irish Close, he went into the final against Rory with mixed emotions but with a very definite plan. "In the afternoon, I was very nervous before the final. There were a lot of people there looking at Rory after his West of Ireland win. He was also half my age, so I made a decision not to look at him and to just concentrate on my own game."

It seemed to be paying dividends when Eddie went one up after the fifth hole, but a little later disaster struck. He lost four in a row and coming to the closing holes found himself four down. Eddie pulled one back when Rory lost a contact lens, but it was only a consolation.

McIlroy soon closed out the match 3&2.

For Eddie, there was disappointment but there was also the realisation that he had lost to the best player he had ever witnessed: "I had never seen anything like his ball striking. I mean, I held true to my plan and did not look at his play until it was nearly over. But I could hear his ball striking and I had never heard, and have still never heard to this day, anything like it.

"I'll put it this way. The sound of his ball striking is amazing. It's the sound of the 'whack' that he makes. It is crisp, clean and it is perfect. It is the same on every single shot he makes.

"Most of us golfers don't fancy playing a 3-iron or 4-iron in the middle of the fairway to the green. He does it naturally, easily and he strikes it beautifully. If there were 20 players striking a ball, and you were blindfolded, you would unquestionably know the sound of Rory's strike."

Now nearing the age of 40 and with a wife, child and job, Eddie still loves the game and plays all the events he can. He never did climb the heights of that day with Rory again, but he admits it is a young, single man's game. He recently joked to fellow players at the Portugese amateur open that he was the only player there to hold all three titles of marriage certificate, christening certificate and RSI number!

But there was one more memory from his tussle with Rory: "The only full shot I allowed myself to watch Rory play came on the 14th. It was a par three and it was very windy. He took out a four-iron and what followed next was unbelievable, and I'll never forget it.

"He played the ball out wide. It seemed to turn in different stages. It was like an old 50 pence coin where it turned to one corner, then another and then another. The ball came in on to the green leaving a chance of a birdie. It was sheer class."

The year of 2006 saw Rory make it back-to-back West of Ireland triumphs when he beat Paul O'Hanlon, of the Curragh, 3&1. O'Hanlon would eventually go on and win the title himself in 2008.

The titles, successes and records kept on coming at a phenomenal rate. After retaining his West of Ireland, Rory travelled to the new Irish Close venue of the European Club to defend that title – and he beat County Louth's Simon Ward 3&2 to retain that championship as well. In so doing, he became the first man to retain his Irish Close title since the legendary Joe Carr recorded three in a row in 1965.

In August 2006 he won the European Amateur Championship at Biella Golf Club, near Milan in Italy, with the score of 274 (65-69-72-68), by three strokes from the Englishman Stephen Lewton.

****

Those first four adult amateur titles won by Rory aged just 15 and 16 represented huge achievements for such a young player. It must be remembered that those titles are not confined to teenagers but cater for golfers of all ages.

At such a young age, and getting better and better, Rory was now really starting to play the kind of golf that his coach Michael Bannon firmly believed was more than good enough to take to the professional European Tour.

Bannon had first laid eyes on Rory as a toddler when, probably just kidding around with him, he gave him a few token lessons and good advice for the future. But later, he took the ten-year-old Rory under his wing at Bangor Golf Club.

As a boy himself, Bannon played the Irish GAA sport of hurling but from the moment his dad Sean, a "leisurely" golfer at his local Kirkistown Golf Club, introduced him to the game of golf, there was only one direction life would take him in. Bannon, inspired by Jack Nicklaus and by watching better players, taught himself the game. It clearly worked very well for him as he reached the final of the 1981 Irish Close Championship before losing to the very gifted Ronan Rafferty.

He was a little similar to Rory – and his parents' protestations were also similar – in that Bannon gave up his day job in a Belfast bank in his early 20s to help his friend Hugh Duggan at Ardglass. From there, he went to Holywood, where Rory was to arrive on the scene.

Bannon continued to make the grade as an accomplished golfer and he actually ended up in a playoff with Padraig Harrington for the 1988 Irish Professional title, but deep down he knew his future was as a coach. In 1999, Gerry McIlroy asked him to teach his gifted son. Bannon's rate was £75 for a 45-minute class. Pretty soon after witnessing Rory's ability, he probably gave him extra tuition at no extra cost, such was his desire to see the young golfer succeed.

In an interview with the *Irish Independent's* golf correspondent Karl McGinty, Bannon said he still had all the early videos of Rory at his teaching facilities in Bangor. But he had first noticed him as a toddler. Rory would be sitting in his buggy watching his dad Gerry practise on the range. Rory picked up everything from his dad – and so quickly.

Bannon revealed how Rory's game is now compared to then: "We've kind of built it up as he grew so it'd always suit Rory at the time he was playing. For example, he had a swing that suited him at ten or 11. Then at 12, he got a bit bigger and we had to fit it a bit.

"At 13, 14 or 15, we looked at it and said, 'this is going well here – there's a few wee things. Maybe your backswing's a bit too around yourself or a bit flat but I think we'll leave it there because you're happy enough at the minute.'"

Bannon added: "I was very lucky because he wanted to learn and just soaked up the information and kind of trusted me all the time. I always knew I was telling him the right things, but you're always kind of nervous. You're thinking is it the right thing for him, is it going to take him to another level?

"Luckily enough, it was. It all just happened that way, through a lot of hard work from himself, mainly, and the fact that Rory's so strong mentally and smart."

When he was 15, as Mick Byrne had seen at Castlebar, Rory was hitting the ball phenomenal distances. Even a coach like Bannon, who had seen it all before, was surprised how far he could hit the ball for his size and his age. "I thought this was fantastic. He was hitting the ball further than a man at that point and he was able to send it out with regular consistency," he recalled.

After leaving school and sweeping up those early amateur titles in the West of Ireland, McIlroy certainly proved that his decision concerning his education was the correct one. This was further endorsed when he leapt to number one in the World Amateur Rankings in the spring of 2007.

After winning the European Amateur Championship in Italy

and receiving the silver medal as leading amateur at that summer's Open Championship at Carnoustie, he officially turned professional following the 2007 Walker Cup in September.

Yet another step up would be required on tour. Bannon was all too aware of this vital fact, and so a lot more intensive coaching sessions were booked for Rory in Bangor. Even as a pro, those sessions have never stopped, as Bannon revealed: "As a professional he started playing more golf, and he had to go up to the next level. Again, there was more responsibility because he's doing this for a living now. So you're biting your nails hoping it's all going to pan out.

"We only changed a couple of little things, which were important but very basic and not massively hard to do, and he's hitting the ball majestically now. The takeaway was great, width at the top of the backswing, balance, strike, everything was in line. As pros, what we look at, everything was there."

Rory's early talent was "frightening", according to Bannon, and he was also a bit of an exhibitionist who loved to show off to the older folk watching.

The very young Rory was so exciting that Bannon found himself impelled to do one very important thing: he had to persuade Holywood Golf Club to allow Rory to join before he reached the age limit of 12! This was no easy task considering the strict rules by which almost all in golf abide. But after explaining his case to the powers that be, Bannon succeeded, as he explained: "Rory was a golfer at the age of eight. You've no idea how good he was. We used to watch him play. He'd say, 'here, look at this,' and you'd have to look and see what he was doing.

"I'd say, 'hey Rory, fade one there,' and next thing he'd hit a lovely wee fade. 'What about a wee hook?' I'd say and he'd ask, 'Do you want a high one or a low one?' You know, he could actually do it."

But what was it that Bannon saw in the young Rory? What made him so different from the thousands of other golfers that he, and many other coaches, have tried to teach golf to over the years?

"They talk about great hands. Well, that's what he had. It was the most amazing thing. He could see the shot and hit it. He knew what to do, straight from the head. Even on the course, he'd say, 'this is how

I see this,' and he'd try to play the shot like that.

"I understand why people want to watch him play – because he's so different. Like Georgie Best or Joey Dunlop or Alex Higgins, there's something in there you can't quantify, you can't quite put your finger on it."

Bannon continued: "It's the X-factor. It's not definable. It's a combination of everything. Like how Georgie Best could take a ball around people and never lose his balance or Joey Dunlop looking like he's part of the bike going around a corner.

"Rory's swing looks great. It flows great and there's great rhythm, stability and balance. But the way the ball is going off the club face is just fantastic. Once I'd watched him play, I wouldn't want to watch anybody else hit the ball, it's so good."

Just as Rory's decision to give up school has been well and truly justified, the sacrifice of giving up the steady day job in the bank has worked well for Bannon. Golf-mad, he is living the dream and has reaped the financial rewards. But like Rory, you get the impression that money simply does not come into the equation.

To have come across a 'once in a lifetime' sporting talent, and to have nurtured his talents from childhood to the present, is much more rewarding, as he says: "To play a lot of golf is very satisfying but I feel very honoured to be able to coach this guy from eight years of age to where he is now. I also feel very humble about it. I sometimes think 'why has this happened to me?' I suppose somebody has to do it!"

Ultimately, Bannon is like the gamekeeper who one day releases the animals he has nurtured back into the wild to fend for themselves. He will watch from afar but in his heart, he will always keep an eye out and he will always be there if help is ever needed. "Rory owns his own swing. He hits the shots. It's not Michael Bannon's golf," he insisted. "I'd say my part as a coach is very much guiding it in the right direction. I'm not just a technical officer.

"I also coach him in the positive side of golf and talk about course management and all that sort of stuff. It's just hard to believe sometimes you're working with potentially the best player in the world."

Chapter 5:
The Ryder Cup Hero

Lee Westwood (England); Rory McIlroy (Northern Ireland); Martin Kaymer (Germany); Graeme McDowell (Northern Ireland); Ian Poulter (England); Ross Fisher (England); Francesco Molinari (Italy); Peter Hanson (Sweden); Miguel Angel Jimenez (Spain); Luke Donald (England); Padraig Harrington (Ireland); Edoardo Molinari (Italy).

It was 29 August 2010, and that was the order in which Ryder Cup captain Colin Montgomerie announced to the world the Europe team that would face the USA at Celtic Manor in Wales. The last three named were Monty's controversial 'wildcard' picks.

The wildcard controversy arose because the FedEx Four, as they were termed – Harrington, Donald, Paul Casey and Justin Rose – chose to stay in America in the last two weeks when returning to Europe could have seen them qualify automatically. Montgomerie was left with one of the toughest decisions any captain ever had to make. He had to leave one of the four out and he also faced calls to omit another because all four had put their US Tour careers ahead of Europe's cause. He had also asked all four to play in the season finale, the Johnny Walker at Gleneagles, and they had all turned him down. Monty had been critical of Poulter for doing the same in advance of the 2008 Ryder Cup.

Of the wildcards he chose, in Harrington's favour was the big plus that he was a three-time major winner. Against him was the fact that he did not win a game in 2008 or in the nine-point massacre of the USA at the K Club in 2006.

Donald's record in Ryder Cups was seen as impeccable. He had lost only one of seven cup games; had a perfect four wins out of four in foursomes; was third at Celtic Manor in the 2010 Wales Open; and was ranked tenth in the world.

Casey was ranked one higher than that and his head-to-head record in matchplay was seen as a huge strength. He had won the World Match Play at Wentworth in 2006 and had been a finalist in two consecutive WGC-Accenture Championships in Arizona. But his luck ran out because he was given a wildcard in 2008 after once again remaining in the States. Another negative against him was his poor Ryder Cup record. So he was overlooked.

Rose had been much more successful with three points out of four on his Ryder Cup debut, partnering Poulter to two wins and also beating the mighty Phil Mickelson in the singles. However, he had played less than anybody in Europe that season and, after two brilliant US Tour victories earlier in the summer of 2010, had missed the halfway cut in the season's last two majors – just like Harrington.

And then there was Edoardo Molinari, whose brother Francesco clinched his debut when England's Ross McGowan pulled out through injury. The pair had also won the World Cup in November 2009 and so they were seen as a rock-solid combination. Against Edoardo, though, was his lack of experience both in majors and in the Ryder Cup – and Montgomerie already had five debutants in McIlroy, Kaymer, Fisher, Francesco Molinari and Hanson.

Out from the last team went Sergio Garcia, Henrik Stenson, Robert Karlsson, Oliver Wilson, Soren Hansen, Casey and Rose – although Garcia did join the team as a fourth vice-captain.

Montgomerie gave the reasons for picking his three wildcards. "Padraig Harrington has won three major championships in the last three years. Padraig also has great stature and we feel that he is a player that nobody in matchplay golf wants to play. He is a great competitor and someone that will bring everything to the team that we know about European golf.

"Luke Donald has played seven times in the Ryder Cup and has lost only once. And Edoardo Molinari, what can one say about his performance today? In my time on the European Tour, over 24 years, I have never seen a finish like that. All credit to him, having to win and doing just that." He was referring to the Italian's barn-storming finish to win the Johnny Walker at Gleneagles.

When Monty was asked about what had counted against Casey and Rose, he responded: "I would rather talk about the strengths of the ones I have picked but I do feel sorry for Paul Casey and Justin Rose. He (Rose) has won twice in the USA this year and is doing well in the Barclays at the moment (he was lying in fifth place). I and my team had to leave out two world stars and I am afraid they are the world stars left out on this occasion."

Although Montgomerie's five debutants were all bracketed in the 'inexperienced' league, there was nothing controversial about Rory McIlroy's place in the team. Being named at number two behind Lee Westwood said it all. Only a year after his maiden Tour win in Dubai, he was an automatic selection in the very first Ryder Cup he had contended for.

Rory's excellent performances had seen him leap up the world points list to the point where he sat just behind Westwood, on 316.95 to Westy's 422.01. In the European Ryder Cup points list, he lay in third place behind Kaymer and the number one, Westwood.

In the build-up to the Ryder Cup, Rory had caused a few little controversies of his own that had made the headlines. Comments he made to various media were leapt upon, and a couple of quotes seemed to suggest the Ryder Cup was over-rated: "If somebody asks me whether I'd rather sink the winning putt in the Ryder Cup or win a major, it's the major every day," he said, adding: "When I was a kid growing up practising, I never had a putt to win the Ryder Cup. I always had a putt to win the Masters or the Open – it's just the way I feel."

He also took a lot of tongue-in-cheek stick from fellow players by referring to the event as an 'exhibition'. But McDowell jumped to his colleague's defence, insisting that Rory would change his mind once he got out to play in the event: "Of course it's different from a major and a WGC – it's not an individual win – it's just something a bit special. It's always been something that's pretty close to my heart. I think when Rory gets out there and feels it next week, he'll maybe have a different view on it."

McIlroy was quickly becoming a tabloid editor's dream. Then he went further and made several comments about Tiger Woods that rebounded all over the world.

Woods had had a turbulent year, with his marriage ending and abysmal form on the course compounding his woes. Just a few weeks before the Ryder Cup, and after Tiger's poor performance at the WGC Bridgestone Invitational, where he had finished 18 over par, McIlroy said: "After what's happened in the last 18 months, I suppose a little bit of that aura is probably gone … Unless his game rapidly improves … I think anyone in the European team would fancy their chances against him.

"Once I met Tiger, even before last year or whatever, you sort of realise that he is just a normal guy. He's probably the best player that's ever lived, and likely the greatest player that's ever played the game.

"But you watch so much golf on TV, and you see so many things and you watch so many highlights … watching Tiger winning the Masters in '97 and winning four majors in a row in 2000/2001, you sort of don't really believe it. You put him on such a high pedestal and then you meet the guy and you realise that he's obviously an unbelievable player, but he's just a normal guy."

When he learned about these quotes – especially Rory saying: "I'd love to face him" – a stern-faced Woods replied: "Me too."

A rather naïve Rory was not to know it, but to those in Ryder Cups always looking for ingredients to stir or rile, these comments just served to add fuel to the fire. But after all the talk, all the hidden riling and all the fanfare, it was time for the real action.

Lee Westwood and Martin Kaymer started proceedings on the morning of Friday, October 1 against the American pairing of Dustin Johnson and Phil Mickelson. That fourball match was followed a few minutes later by McIlroy's debut.

Rory and his compatriot Graeme McDowell faced Stewart Cink and Matt Kuchar. The American pair were first up on the tee. Both drove their balls into the rough. McDowell hit a perfect drive down the middle, but there was to be a shaky start from Rory, who also found the rough. Cink and Kuchar just hacked out on to the fairway while Rory caught the greenside bunker. McDowell found the green.

Two putts for par were enough for McDowell and Europe were 1up. By the fourth hole, they were still 1up, with McDowell on fire. After getting plugged in a bunker and finding another bunker, he played a majestic third shot to inches from the pin for par.

That was when the rains came, with some of the worst weather ever witnessed at a Ryder Cup. It was miserable and it was monsoon-like. The match was suspended at 9.45am and did not resume until 5pm that evening.

At the time, Europe could not have wished for a better start. Rory and Graeme were in the lead while up ahead, Westwood and Kaymer were 4up after six holes. Behind them, the situation made even better reading. Ross Fisher and Ian Poulter were 1up on the powerful pairing of Tiger Woods and Steve Stricker after three holes. However, Padraig Harrington and Luke Donald were behind and struggling in their match with Jeff Overton and Bubba Watson.

The situation soon changed for the Northern Irish. In a seesaw match, the Yanks fought back and went 2up at the 11th hole. Despite a brilliant McIlroy shot there, he missed a five-foot putt and that was symptomatic of his struggle throughout. He was finding the rough, the water and a good number of bunkers.

Then, as America went 2up, play was suspended for the day as darkness covered the course. It resumed again at 8am the next morning, Saturday.

What a difference a night makes; Rory came back on the Saturday a totally different player. He pulled a hole back for the Europeans on the 13th when a great shot to the green spun back to three feet. The crowds went wild and the smile was back on Rory's face.

The only show in the Welsh valleys was Rory McIlroy. He faced tough pressure putts on the next hole and on the 15th but he made them both. But he was saving his very best for the penultimate hole.

On the par three 17th, McDowell played a beautiful iron to within 15 feet of the pin. It was a great birdie chance for Europe, but Rory made poor contact and was all of 30 feet from the hole. Both Americans had good birdie chances.

As he was the furthest from the hole, Rory stepped forward to putt first. There then followed an explosion of noise that echoed through every valley, telling Wales and Europe that Rory had birdied. Cink and Kuchar missed and Rory had saved the day. At the second last hurdle he had put in a fine effort to draw level with the leaders.

Although he found the water on the last hole, McDowell stepped up to the mark and the match ended in a half. It was Rory's very first score in his very first Ryder Cup match – albeit a half point.

By the end of the fourballs, however, Europe were behind, trailing the USA by 2.5 – 1.5 pts. Westwood/Kaymer had beaten Cink/Kuchar but Harrington/Donald had lost to Watson/Overton. Meanwhile, the much talked of Tiger Woods had won his match with Steve Stricker against Ian Poulter and Ross Fisher.

It was not the start Europe had been hoping for, and the weather was also the subject of much debate. Following some of the worst weather ever witnessed at a golf event, never mind the Ryder Cup, some people were furious and even embarrassed considering all the marketing and tourism effort that goes into this hugely prestigious event, there were calls for changes to its organisation. Some suggested the idea of holding the Ryder Cup in the autumn in northern Europe should be looked at seriously. Players and spectators alike were walking the course freezing and wet.

The delays had caused a lot of hassle but at that time there was another very real worry. If the weather did not relent, there was the very real possibility that the 2010 Ryder Cup could be cancelled.

The calendar might have shown that northern Europe was just out of September and into October, but in reality the conditions made it look like the coldest and wettest day of the decade. Those who were calling for a Ryder Cup calendar change seemed to have a case.

****

Samuel Ryder was an English seed merchant and entrepreneur from St Albans in Hertfordshire who made his money selling penny seed packets. When he took up golf late in life to improve his health, he enlisted Abe Mitchell as his personal tutor.

Ryder was so fascinated and delighted to see Mitchell and George Duncan defeat defending Open champion Jim Barnes and the great Walter Hagen, at Wentworth in 1926, that he was heard to say in the 19th hole: "We must do this again."

So it was that one of the world's greatest sporting events was born. Ryder donated a gold cup as part of the prize. It cost £250 and the small golfing figure at the top of the trophy stands as a lasting memorial to Abe Mitchell.

The first 22 Ryder Cup matches pitched Great Britain and Ireland against the United States, with the US winning 18, GB and Ireland claiming three and one match, the famous 1969 contest, being tied. In 1979, GB & Ireland became Europe, with Seve Ballesteros and Antonio Garrido becoming the first continental golfers to play in the tournament. In the subsequent 15 matches, Europe and the US had each won seven, with one match tied.

On home soil, Europe were desperate to go back in front again, but after the fourballs things were not looking good. And they did not look any better when Friday's foursomes were completed. The Stricker/Woods duo hammered Jimenez/Hanson 4&3; Johnson/Mahan beat the Molinari brothers in a very close match 2up; while Furyk/Fowler halved their match with Westwood/Kaymer. Although it was still early days, it was looking bad for Europe. The USA were leading 5-2 and, with three matches remaining, the Europeans needed to do something.

When Harrington/Fisher beat Mickelson/Johnson 3&2 and Poulter/Donald held on to beat Watson/Overton 2&1, suddenly it was game on again. Europe now trailed 5-4 with McIlroy/McDowell v Cink/Kuchar the last match left on the course.

Little did they know it then, but two of the four, namely McIlroy and Cink, would eventually go on to play out a defining moment in that 2010 Ryder Cup. As it was, all four were involved in a titanic tussle right to the end of the second session.

Matt Kuchar struck the first blow for the Americans when he holed for birdie from ten feet on the second. After Europe squared the match at the third, Rory's beautiful chip and run to within a few feet of the pin at the fourth put Europe 1up.

When the lead changed hands on two more occasions before the halfway stage, word filtered around the course that this match was becoming a nailbiting classic. Then, after squaring the match at the tenth, the Americans went in front at the 12th. Kuchar again showed a touch of brilliance and it seemed as if the USA now held the advantage with holes running out. On the next however, Rory nailed his ten-foot birdie and as Cink missed his, they were level again.

The crowds who joined in were not to be disappointed as, over the remaining holes, the drama intensified. Unbelievably, Europe, from one down on the 13th, went 1up after the 15th as McDowell was the only one to find the green.

With just three holes left, Europe had fought back and shown huge courage and character to lead. This was typical Ryder Cup and the sort of stuff that Samuel witnessed back in 1926 to inspire this great event. If McIlroy and McDowell could hold their nerve, they would lead Europe into the third session level at 5-5.

Rory stepped up to drive on the 16th tee. All eyes were on him. The other three waited their turn while the huge crowds bobbed and wove for a view. But nerves were about to hit every one of the golfers assembled at the tee. McIlroy shook his head as his ball found the rough. Cink also found the rough stuff while Kuchar was so deep in it that his ball was lucky to be found.

But McDowell also found the thick stuff and after a catalogue of errors, it was the Yanks who squared the match once more. Two holes were left and you could hear a pin drop. In such silence, McIlroy and McDowell could hear their heartbeats thundering in their ears.

Very often when the chips are down, moments of sheer class and brilliance manifest themselves. This 17th hole was about to become an all-time classic, one that will long live in the memory.

The green played almost 200 yards, so it was a testing little par three. Kuchar stepped up and played safe to the centre of the green. Then it was the turn of McDowell. With a 5-iron, he went straight at the flag to bellows of "in the hole". He liked it. His eyes popped out of his head as he watched the flight. The whole golf course erupted into roars as the ball landed five feet from the pin.

There were 'high-fives' from the Northern Ireland pair and Europe were smiling. However, there were those who did not like the celebrations –in particular those from Rory. In his moment of excitement, he could have spurred on the Americans, they thought. Mark Reason, at Celtic Manor for the *Telegraph*, wrote: "There was a naivety about the 21-year-old in his afternoon foursomes. When playing partner Graeme McDowell hit a superb shot to five foot at the penultimate hole, McIlroy wound up the moment with a flashy celebration. The kid has not watched enough Ryder Cups. You sensed it would fire Cink into a killing response."

While Rory waited to knock in the short putt, thanks to G-Mac's moment of magic, Cink and his caddie took their time and surveyed their long putt. It was tricky, with a left to right break, and it was downhill to boot. And Cink made it! There was a moment of delight and fist clenching, quickly ceasing as the Americans returned to the sobering thought of Europe going ahead once again in one of the greatest foursomes matches in history.

McIlroy stepped forward for the winning of the hole. Seconds later he was holding his head in his hands. He had missed! The putt lipped out and from Europe looking assured of going 1up, it was the USA who hit the front as they approached the final hole.

Only in the Ryder Cup could you have such moments, with four players producing high drama on the same hole and at the same time. It was real breathtaking stuff and it made the miserable weather recede into the background. Safe play from Kuchar; a brilliant stone-dead shot from McDowell; a fantastic putt from Cink; and then a seemingly disastrous slip-up from Rory. Europe had to do something at the last hole. Could they haul themselves back from the brink one more time?

They got off to a good start on the 18th. After Cink had found the rough, McIlroy composed himself and made the fairway. But he and McDowell then found sand and that was the end. The Americans won a titanic duel by two holes, and they led the tournament by 6-4.

After a very promising start from McIlroy on his Ryder Cup debut, missing that short putt had been a cruel blow. Now he had to pick himself up, and this time not for himself, but for the team – for Europe.

Captain Montgomerie did not let Rory mull over the missed opportunity. He picked McDowell and McIlroy to come out again and play in the third session foursomes, behind the opening pairing of Westwood/Donald.

And Europe got off to a cracking start in their bid to close the gap on the Americans. 'Westy' and Donald were never in danger as they tore Woods and Stricker apart to win 6&5. It was another point on the board for the Europeans and the score was now 6-5 to the USA.

Coming up behind the victorious Westwood and Donald, McIlroy and McDowell were not having a very easy time in their match. Zach Johnson and Hunter Mahan were proving formidable opponents.

Things looked to be going well for the Irish pair when they found themselves 3up by the seventh. But when the US pair cut the gap to 2down with two holes to play, it was another tense time for Europe. Then a combination of luck and brilliance finished off the match in Europe's favour.

Mahan's tee shot on the par three 17th bounced to the left, but the ball was running towards the hole. It looked as though the American pairing might get lucky and take the match to the final hole. But the ball kept on rolling until it went off the green.

McDowell's ball found the green and stayed up. When Rory stepped forward and sank it for a birdie the Irishmen had won the match 3&1, but they celebrated as if they had won the Euromillions. Rory said: "To get that first win under my belt in the Ryder Cup is fantastic and to do it alongside this guy [McDowell] is even more special. He's been great for me this week and it's made my life a lot easier walking the fairways with him."

The match score was now tied at 6-6. It had been the perfect reply from Europe and attention now turned towards the fourballs later that afternoon.

Emotionally and physically drained by their two previous match experiences as they were, it was not surprising that McIlroy and McDowell were given the rest of the day off. Not that they were going anywhere other than the course, to support the rest of the team!

It would turn out to be an unforgettable day. Padraig Harrington and Ross Fisher, the first pairing out, beat Dustin Johnson and Jim Furyk 2&1, and the result kick-started a day of complete European dominance. Their win was followed by further victories for Hanson/ Jimenez over Watson/Overton and for Poulter/Kaymer over Mickelson/Fowler. In the other fourball, the Molinari brothers fought back from under the cosh to earn an unlikely looking half-point against Cink and Kuchar.

The Americans were well and truly sunk. When the day ended, they had been stuffed in five of the six matches. Cink/Kuchar had prevented a complete whitewash with their half-point, but the entire picture had now changed so dramatically. Trailing 6-4 after the second session, Europe had won the third session 5.5 – 0.5 pt.

In press conferences, Monty insisted his team were not counting any chickens and there was still a lot of work to do. Off camera, though, the Europeans were cock-a-hoop, patting themselves on the back for turning the match around and into a great victory. The scoreline justified the self-congratulation, but nobody could have predicted what was to unfold.

****

Going into the final day's singles matches in the 2010 Ryder Cup, Europe held a 9.6 – 6.5 pts lead. To win, the Americans would need to win seven of the 12 singles and take a half from one of the other five in the fourth session.

It was possible but highly improbable. Perhaps if they had been playing on their own soil in front of a partisan and vociferous crowd, it might have been likely. But it was Europe who now had the momentum, and they just needed four wins and a half from 12 singles.

However, there was a precedent: a comeback of even greater magnitude. Ben Crenshaw's US team had come from 10-6 down in 1999 to beat Europe 14.4 – 13.5 in what was called the Miracle at Brookline. So there was hope for the Yanks, but it was a daunting task.

You can have one guess as to who Rory was paired against in the singles. After having had it rammed it down his throat on the 17th once already, he would face Stewart Cink again. Monty put

Lee Westwood out first followed by Rory, Luke Donald and Martin Kaymer. He backed that up by putting Harrington out second last and McDowell out as last man.

As events unfolded, it was close in the top three games. However, Dustin Johnson was powering his way to an effortless win against Kaymer in game four. When Steve Stricker beat Westwood 2&1, things were starting to get just a little tense. A pumped-up Cink was, at times, handing out harsh lessons to Rory and the third match, between Donald and Furyk, was level. So the Americans were making a pretty good fist of it.

In matches five and seven, Poulter and Jimenez were comfortably ahead. But with the Molinari brothers, Peter Hanson and Harrington all struggling, all of a sudden things were getting a little bit too close for comfort. America were up in six of the 12 singles and several of the others were in the balance. In the event, Rory's match with Cink would become the most significant of all – even more so than the games involving McDowell and Edoardo Molinari.

There was a fantastic atmosphere as McIlroy and Cink made their way to the first tee. The crowd were fully expecting Europe to win on this day, and they were in high spirits. "You've got Big Mac, we've got Little Mac," they chanted. The support no doubt spurred McIlroy on as he raced to 2up after the first two holes. But not to be outdone, the big balding American won the next three in a row to go 1up.

Rory squared the match at the sixth before Cink regained control at the eighth, and he held the advantage until a piece of McIlroy magic at the 12th. Cink found the bunker from 160 yards while Rory, with a 9-iron from 150 yards, spun the ball back to six inches to win the hole.

But disaster struck for Rory on the next. After the ball had spun back beautifully on the previous hole, it spun back again on the par three 13th. This time it found the water. Cink just played the percentages and knocked it on the green to win the hole.

It had been another enormous Ryder Cup struggle so far. It seems that every match is in that competition. But on the balance of overall play, Cink probably just about deserved to be in front. At times, his all-round greater experience was showing to good effect. Then, on the 15th, Rory's dogged determination won the day. His opponent's

Teen prodigy Rory
McIlroy turned pro on
September 18th 2007

Rory had his first win
on the European Tour
in 2009

Rory during a practice
round of the PGA
Championship

Rory employs the interlocking grip on full shots

Rory's sublime swing as taught to him by local pro and coach Michael Bannon

Rory has been cited as one of the most exciting young prospects in golf

Rory & Lee Westwood are both handled by Chubby Chandler's International Sports Management

Rory's friends and mentors include Northern Ireland players Graeme McDowell & Darren Clarke

Rory uses a Scotty
Cameron putter

Rory has recently obtained putting instruction from Dave Stockton

The crowds follow Rory wherever he plays

Rory with the victorious European Ryder Cup Team

Ryder Cup, Celtic
Manor, 2010

Rory wins US Open
by eight shots

The very scenic
Holywood Clubhouse

The town entrance on the outer
suburbs of Belfast and banner
Rory captured on his mobile

Holywood, proud to be the home of
Rory McIlroy 2011 US Open Champion

Welcome to
HOLYWOOD

undoubted brilliance was undone by a failure to enforce his authority and ram it home.

Cink blasted to the front of the green and the ball landed within 15 feet. Rory found the bunker. It was very much advantage Cink in the match: if he won this hole he would have a two-hole advantage with only three left.

Incredibly, McIlroy found a good line from the sand and got his ball to within two feet of the hole. The crowd went ballistic and Cink sportingly acknowledged his opponent's shot. And it must have rattled the American as, unbelievably, he three-putted to hand Rory the hole.

And that's the way it remained for the last three holes, with Rory inspired and, in the end, Cink hanging on for the half. From looking as if he would go two down, Rory had squared the match, and the significance would soon become clear.

When Edoardo Molinari battled back to square his match, it all came down to the last pairing on the course, between Graeme McDowell and Hunter Mahan. With the scores tied 13.5 – 13.5, Rory – and the rest of the golf course – rushed to support Graeme.

In one of the most amazing Ryder Cups, the Americans now had the bit between their teeth. The unthinkable was coming to fruition. The scores were tied and Mahan was playing very well in the final game, with scores tied.

McDowell, who had at one time been struggling against the American, then found a sudden burst of inspiration, no doubt swept up in the immense tide of emotion willing and pushing him on. Some terrific long-range putts on the last few holes sealed an unforgettable win by 3&1 and Europe went wild. It was a valiant effort by Pavin and his troops and Mahan, inconsolable, later blamed himself for submitting to the European euphoria.

McIlroy had never seen anything like it. He joined in the celebrations with his team as the champagne corks popped and the flags flew. Rory admitted he was now a huge Ryder Cup fan, as Sandy Macaskill in the *Telegraph* wrote: "The 21-year-old, his hair still wet with champagne, said that the shivers going through him on a nailbiting final day signalled that this was an experience he would never forget, despite past proclamations. Completely caught up in the moment, he trumpeted that he did not want to miss one of these from now until his 40s.

"'This has been the best week of my golfing life, by far," the Northern Irishman said. 'It's been absolutely incredible. To share every moment with these guys up on stage, it's just been fantastic.

"'And you know, I'm still very, very young, and I don't want to miss a Ryder Cup for the next 20 years. And I certainly don't want to be watching the one in two years' time on telly.'

"This is the player who last year described the Ryder Cup as just an exhibition. The one who, in the innocence of youth, had played the whole thing down.

"It couldn't possibly be that important, could it? But as soon as he strode on to the first tee with McDowell on Friday, he caught the bug. 'It's the best exhibition, isn't it?' cracked Lee Westwood.

"'It's the best exhibition in the world,' McIlroy replied. 'It's been fantastic,' he added. 'You know, I realise now what the Ryder Cup means and how much it means to everyone, and I'm a big fan.'"

"Who could blame him? He had holed his putt on the 18th from five feet to secure what turned out to be an all-important half point against Stewart Cink.

Eyes shining, he delivered the killer line: 'And you know, I truly believe that this is the best golf tournament in the world.'"

Chapter 6:
The Nightmare of 2008

Thursday, 20 September 2007 was a momentous day for Rory McIlroy. It was the day he played in the British Masters but, more importantly, it was the day he made his European Tour debut as a professional golfer.

Previously that year, he had played in three Tour events as an amateur. On February 1 he played in his second consecutive Dubai Desert Classic, in which he finished tied 52nd after rounds of 69, 69, 71 and 76, behind the winner Henrik Stenson.

Rory also missed his second cut on Tour. On April 12, rounds of 77 and 73 meant a swift exit from the Spanish Open. As an amateur playing the Open Championship, he also finished tied 42nd after opening up with a first round of 68.

Rory earned his chance at the professional ranks by qualifying from the Tour School at the Oxfordshire. After finishing on eight under par, he ended up in 13th position, which gained him entry to the last four events of the season on the Tour proper.

But to avoid having to go back to the European Qualifying School or playing the Challenge Tour to gain his full tour card, Rory had to amass £150,000 winnings. If he could earn that amount from those last few events of 2007, he would qualify for the 2008 Tour.

He started with a very good under-par round of 69 but then shot a disastrous 78 in his second round. He then steadied the ship somewhat with final rounds of 70 and 73. Coincidentally, he finished in the same position as his last amateur event in the Open – tied 42nd.

His very first cheque on the European Tour amounted to €15,128. It was minuscule compared to Lee Westwood's first prize of €435,000, but it was a start and Rory had a chance to increase that when he played a prestigious event two weeks later. The Alfred Dunhill Links Championship would also give him invaluable experience of playing some Open golf courses. The event was played over a variety of golf courses including the Old Course at St Andrews and Carnoustie.

England's Nick Dougherty won that event and with it a huge prize of €563,000. But Rory enjoyed a fantastic tournament and he ended up in third position, just three shots behind the winner. With rounds of 71, 67, 67 and 68, he ended up -15 for the event. In only his second event as a pro, he had guaranteed his Tour Card for the 2008 season after winning €211,000.

At the Madeira Island Open on October 14, he finished tied fourth behind Denmark's Mads Vibe-Haustrup to pick up another €42,000. Then, in his final event of the season, he tied 56th in the Portugal Masters to add another €9,000 to his bank balance.

All the promise he had shown as an amateur was coming to fruition. He had made the cut in all four events he had played as a professional. A third place finish together with two top tens had brought his earnings to just over €277,000. Of much more importance, though, was the fact that he could now play as a fully fledged professional in 2008.

McIlroy could not have wished for a better start and it was easy to see why people like Andrew 'Chubby' Chandler had snapped him up so eagerly. The majority of seasoned golfers play all year. Rory, in the small window of just a few events, had finished 95th on the money list.

The world was his oyster. If he could manage to achieve what he had achieved in just four season-ending tournaments, what could he do in a full season? It was no surprise that so many people expected

Rory to win his first event on the 2008 European Tour.

The start of a European golf season actually begins at the end of the previous year, with events mostly played in South Africa, Asia or Australasia. So, just before Christmas, on 13 December 2007, Rory McIlroy began his first full season as a professional, teeing off in the South African Airways Open.

His debut season quickly turned into a baptism of fire. The long trip proved in vain as Rory opened up with one of his worst ever career rounds. An 83 meant that he had to ring the airport to tell them he would be returning home in two days. A second round 74 was irrelevant.

Returning home a few days later with his tail between his legs, Rory must have been embarrassed. A first round score of +11 had the appearance of an eyesore, and the blow was such that Rory extended his Christmas at home. While his Northern Ireland chums Darren Clarke and Michael Hoey returned to South Africa just after Christmas for the Joburg Open, McIlroy did not make his second start until January 17.

Jetting to the United Arab Emirates for the Abu Dhabi Golf Championship, he started poorly once again. He shot a first round of 73 but improved steadily over the next three days. With scores of 71, 69 and 68 he finished in a share of 11th place and picked up a nice cheque for €21,500. It was the perfect boost for his image and, above all, his confidence.

Rory remained in the Gulf States to play in the Qatar Masters a week later. A third round of 66 was the highlight of his week but either side of that were some mediocre and bad rounds. Ending up at -6 for the week, he tied 33rd and credited another €12,000 to his account. It was early days, but Rory was struggling. The signs were obvious that he was finding consistency hard to come by.

Popping across to Dubai a few days later, he would surely be inspired by the arrival of Tiger Woods for the Dubai Desert Classic. Tiger repaid the organisers for their faith and money invested in him by winning, but Rory was not around to see it. Incredibly, he missed his second cut in just four events of the new season – after opening up with a promising 69, he shot a second round 77. It was another early flight home and more worry about the huge inconsistencies between rounds.

Now it was crisis time. A golfer touted with as big a future as Rory simply had to find out what was going wrong. In the heat and pressure of it all, with sponsors and management teams looking on anxiously, he simply had to take time out.

While Graeme McDowell and Darren Clarke spent most of the next four weeks tagging along with the Tour through Asia, Rory took six weeks off. But when he returned on March 13, it got even worse.

McDowell won the Ballantines Championship on Jeju Island in South Korea, but for his fellow Ulsterman it was yet another missed cut. He must have felt like sending out flares and an SOS from the island. His cries were heard and he was swiftly taken out and home before McDowell popped the champagne corks. Yet another first round debacle had proved to be his undoing, and that 76 was followed by a 71.

Another two-week break followed before Rory returned, in the Andalucian Open. On this occasion he started brightly with a four under par round of 68, but from there he regressed with two bad rounds of 73 and 74. He took home a paltry €6,000.

A week later at the Portugal Open in Estoril, on April 3, he showed vastly improved form and strung three great rounds together. Scores of 69, 67 and 66 even put him in with a chance of winning, but a final round of 71 slipped him to a tie for 15th on 11 under par. Nevertheless, perhaps this was the kick-start McIlroy had been searching for.

A break for the US Masters ensued, so Rory did not play again for three weeks. When he did, it was in that popular destination for Northern Ireland golfers – Asia.

Not so popular for Rory. By the time his tournament finished he must have been sick of the sight of the continent. His buddy Darren Clarke won the BMW Asian Open in Shanghai but Rory opened up with two 73s and finished with a 76.

He took another three weeks off, his mind now obviously in turmoil. There had to be some physical or psychological reason for his poor form. There was no other explanation. Shooting high 70s and even an 83 was just not Rory McIlroy.

****

Could Adare Manor, the venue for his beloved Irish Open, provide the perfect pick-me-up? That is what all Irish golf fans and writers were now asking themselves. Nobody took any pleasure in seeing a gifted young golfer struggle.

There is something unique about Irish sports fans – not just golf fans. There is an in-built sense of fair play in their psyche and so, when they see a competitor struggling, they try to lift him or her. If a cyclist falls to the ground in the Tour de France, they rush to the scene to see if he is all right. It is in their nature to help him back up and see him off with an encouraging push.

Rory must have sensed all the goodwill towards him. For the first time in months, he was playing in his own backyard. He felt very much at home and it showed in his demeanour. The old Rory smile was back and he transmitted it right through Adare.

Despite not hitting a round under 70, he finished at six under par and on his own in seventh place. Three rounds of 70 and a level par 72 earned him a first top ten finish of the season and a handsome cheque for €75,000.

At Wentworth the following week, however, he was brought back down to earth. Another missed cut showed that the inconsistencies were still there in his game. Rounds of 74 and 77 meant he had to pack his bags and prepare for Wales the very next week.

Without setting the valleys alight, he produced steady enough golf. Opening with a 68, he at least managed to avoid an over-par round. Another 68 on the par 70 course meant he finished -5 and tied 39th.

After a near three-week break, Rory flew to Munich for the prestigious BMW Championship, and the frustration returned once more. He must have felt like tearing his hair out when he failed, yet again, to make the weekend. A level par 72 was followed by a second round 75. Things were now becoming even more serious. In fact, it was becoming embarrassing. A golfer tipped to become one of the world's best had now missed five cuts from 12 events.

That quickly became six from 13 at the French Open on June 26, following two more rounds in the 70s. As he flew to England the following week, Rory was no doubt hoping and praying that his situation could only improve. But after some respite, it was only going to get worse.

Kent Golf Club in England staged the European Open and Rory began very well with a 67. That was more like it, and he now had the perfect platform from which to hit another few rounds in the 60s and challenge for the title.

Alas, the same old problem returned. Rounds of 71, 72 and 74 saw him gradually slip down the leaderboard. One small consolation was the fact that his opening round was still good enough for a joint tenth place finish and another nice cheque for €54,000.

On the bonnie banks of Loch Lomond a week later, McIlroy put in something of an erratic display. Two rounds in the high 60s and two in the 70s saw him finish -5 and in a tie for 19th. At least a top ten and a top 20 had given hope that he might finally reach a bit of consistency.

Those hopes were to be dashed and Rory would be stung by an unbelievable sequence of events. After a break of some four weeks, he arrived in Stockholm, Sweden for the SAS Masters – and missed the cut with two rounds of 71.

In Holland a week later, he did not wait around to see Darren Clarke win his second Tour title of the season. Clarke added the Dutch Open to his earlier win in Shanghai. McIlroy missed the cut again.

The misery turned into a nightmare three-in-a-row of missed cuts in Scotland the following week. At the Johnny Walker Championship in Gleneagles, Rory brought his missed cuts statistics to 50 per cent – nine from 18 events – and he was now in a deep, dark place.

No doubt he practised, practised and practised but it was not working. His game seemed to have all the parts there but joining them together was the problem. There simply had to be something wrong on the mental side of his game. Intensive sessions with a sports psychologist must surely have been required. Rory's game was falling apart because all the knocks and disappointments were having an adverse effect on his mind, which in turn was having a detrimental effect on his game.

The seemingly never-ending chain of events took another twist on September 4. At the Omega European Masters in Switzerland, he opened up with a superb and almost flawless 63. However, it was followed by one of the greatest blows of his career.

Rounds of 71, 66 and 71 followed and he ended the tournament on -13 and tied at the top with French player Jean-Francois Lucquin. It was the first playoff of Rory's career, but he should already have wrapped up his first Tour win at the 72nd hole. His par attempt from five feet at the last failed and he angrily threw his ball into the water by the green. A par would have meant that at 19, he would have become the third youngest European Tour winner in history. As it stood, he was now entering that sudden-death playoff with Lucquin.

McIlroy had another chance to win on the first extra hole when both players went down the 18th again. But his 15-foot attempt missed and, even then, worse was to follow.

Playing the 405-yard 18th for the third time, he hit a 25-foot birdie putt two feet past the cup and incredibly, he missed that too. Lucquin, 12 feet away, suddenly had two putts to lift his first European Tour title in 175 attempts. He sank his first attempt. The 29-year-old, who was residing in Switzerland, had been ranked 460th in the world at the start of the tournament. For McIlroy, the runner's up cheque of €222,000, plus a €5,000 wristwatch for his first round 63, were little consolation. He was dejected.

"Obviously I am very disappointed," he said. "I got very unlucky on the 18th in regulation, where it got a pretty big bounce for a sand wedge. I hit a good chip, but not a very good putt. Then second time around in the playoff it didn't really matter as he holed his.

"That made me feel a bit better after missing that putt. I can take a lot from this week – I played very well all week and played well coming down the stretch, but unfortunately one bad shot cost me."

Rory continued: "I came here after three missed cuts in a row and found a bit of form. It would have been nice to go home with the trophy, but I have plenty more tournaments even this year. It would be great to get a win this year, but if not I have the rest of my career. C'est la vie."

No matter how poor Rory glossed it over, the title had been there for him to take. And he had blown it. He had been four clear going into the final round but, after bogeys at the second and third, he had suddenly found himself one behind and then down to fourth place at one point.

However, he showed great grit and determination in battling back from that and moving one ahead again by sinking a 20-foot birdie putt at the long 15th.By getting down in a chip and a putt on the next two holes he had stood on the last needing par to win. Going through the green gave Lucquin hope but after Rory's magnificent chip had run just past the edge of the hole, he was one shot from glory. But he had missed that putt. The rest was forgettable.

But that stinging defeat spurred Rory on to his finest and most consistent period of golf since the form he had displayed at the end of 2007 in the 'famous four' events. He was in blistering form and made three top tens from his next four events – all played weekly.

At last he was showing the sort of form that everybody had come to expect from him when he joined the Tour. Then, in the fifth event at the Volvo Masters, he disappointed with four rounds in the mid-70s. Perhaps fatigue had set in after a month of play and travel.

So a three-week break followed before Rory flew to Hong Kong on November 20 for the Hong Kong Open. After opening with another 70, he followed it with great rounds of 64 and 66 to put him in with a great chance of winning.

In the final round, his excellent form continued and a 65 looked like it might be good enough but, amazingly, he was to end up in yet another playoff. This time, though, he was to face two others: Lin Wen-Tang of Chinese Taipei and Francesco Molinari of Italy. Still, he had another chance to create that little bit of history.

Molinari could only par the first playoff hole on the par four 18th while Lin and McIlroy both birdied, meaning the two would face off again.

McIlroy sent his tee shot into a crowd of spectators to the left of the fairway but recovered by hitting his approach shot on to the edge of the green. Lin, meanwhile, hit the fairway from the tee before superbly hitting his second shot to within a foot of the pin and, when McIlroy failed to putt for a birdie, the 34-year-old applied the easy finish to become the first Asian in a decade to win the tournament.

It is hard to know who was in the worse predicament: Padraig Harrington, who endured something like 30-odd runner-up positions, or Rory McIlroy losing two playoffs in three months in his quest for a first title. What is certain is that a new and more resilient McIlroy had risen from the ashes, judging by his reaction afterwards.

"As long as I can keep putting myself in these positions and feeling the nerves and the adrenaline, I'll know I'm doing things right," he said. "It's been a great week and I can't be too disappointed. That's the way it goes. I'll be able to pull through sooner or later and I still have two events left in South Africa."

Judging by that quote, in the immediate aftermath of his Hong Kong loss, he seemed to have accepted the situation, with a firm view to moving forwards. His backroom team had obviously been working on instilling a new-found confidence and resolve.

The results from those final two South African events reflected Rory's entire year. In the first one, he missed the cut and in his last event, the South African Open, he tied third.

That tournament ended a couple of days before Christmas, and it could not have come at a better time. It was time to get home to family and a time to regroup, refocus and recharge the batteries; there was also New Year resolution to make and keep: find that so far elusive first win.

Chapter 7:
Realising Dreams

A new year and a brand new start for Rory. He had to get on and refocus ahead of his second full season on Tour. The pain and the hurt of the previous year were now history. But amid all that heartache, there was some sweet consolation for him.

Despite only making 16 cuts out of 27 and losing out in two playoffs the previous season, the prize money had lifted him into Europe's top 50. A total of €700,000 gave him a finishing position of 36th on the money list, which meant plenty of lucrative invitations.

Organisers of some of the most prestigious events and majors would now be inviting Rory to their events. When he was told after his second playoff defeat in Hong Kong that he had secured an invite to the US Masters, he said: "That puts me in a great position going into the new year."

Abu Dhabi on January 15, for the Abu Dhabi Championship, was Rory's first port of call in 2009. He could not have wished for a better start: a first round 66 gave him the perfect launchpad for an assault on that title.

He followed it up with a 69 but a third round 71 stopped him in his tracks and he lost ground on the leaders. A magnificent final score of 65, his best of the week, was not enough and he came up short. On -17, he finished four shots behind the winner, Paul Casey.

Nevertheless, it was a solid start to his season. Three great rounds had been scuppered by an ordinary third outing, which could have cost him victory. In the end, he tied fifth.

A week later, Rory travelled to Qatar for the Qatar Masters, but a bad opening round had him on the back foot from the start. A 76 meant he was staring down the barrel of another missed cut. A top ten finish followed by another M/C was definitely not what he wanted.

Packing his bags early would have been a huge setback and might have set in motion a similar pattern to that of the previous year. What was of crucial importance, though, was the fact that he wished to stay in that part of the world for his booking in Dubai the week after.

The next day, Rory's battling 68 just helped him to survive the halfway mark, but it was a close shave. With final rounds of 70 and 71 he finished the event just inside the top 50 and with a cheque for €10,000.

In the Dubai Desert Classic on February 29, he opened with a fantastic eight under par 64. It was his best showing in three events, and it also showed that he was in pretty good form. This was two shots better than his opening score in Abu Dhabi, and he was now in pole position to win.

The big question was: could he really put the opposition to the sword by stringing another few low rounds together? If he could, his first title was tangibly close, but previously there had always been one average round that had ruined his chances of winning a title.

Rory turned the screw tighter in his bid for a maiden Tour win the next day, when he shot 68. Then he effectively put one hand on the trophy by going even better the following day with 67. The leaderboard showed -17 after three rounds: a score good enough to win a title, but there was still one more day to go.

In the last round, yet another prize seemed to be slipping through Rory's fingers as five consecutive birdies around the turn were cancelled out by three straight bogeys on the back nine. He then shot through the final green into a bunker but rescued the situation by chipping up to within three feet. Later, he would rate that shot as the best sand-save he has ever played.

Justin Rose had a chance to force at least a playoff with a 15-foot birdie putt but he missed, allowing McIlroy to secure par from four feet for victory. Rory had scrambled to a one-shot win.

Good job, then, that his mediocre round had come on the final day. In normal circumstances, a 70 would probably not have been good enough but the impressive scoring of his previous rounds had done enough. Rose's 67 bore testimony to that.

At long last, Rory McIlroy had become a champion on the European Tour. Throughout his amateur days, while winning everything that was put in front of him, he had dreamt of just such a day. The amateur successes had led to this day, and this day would hopefully lead to the majors.

For the moment, however, he savoured every second of what he had just achieved. The beaming Rory smile was back. The waves of curly black locks were drenched in champagne. It was his greatest day as a professional.

Later, he said: "You watch it on TV and you see guys coming down the stretch with a four- or five-shot lead, you think it's easy, but it's not. You still have to play the shots and hole the putts. I got myself into a great position in the middle of the back nine, but Justin fought back. But it was nice to hold it together on the last and get a great up and down."

That victory moved Rory up 15 places to number 14 in the world rankings and to number two in the Race to Dubai. He now savoured playing four events on the US Tour before his boyhood dream of playing in the Masters. Reflecting on these achievements, he said: "This win has definitely moved me up a step and I just want to keep getting better and better. Your success only makes you more motivated to do better. I have become a very good player, but I still have a lot of years to progress and I just want to keep improving and hopefully one day I will be able to compete with Tiger [Woods]."

The pain, agony and embarrassment of 2008 were now replaced by the sheer delight and joy of winning that first professional tournament. After all the hard work and perseverance, his persistence had paid off. Looking back, he could now acknowlege the relief: "It's definitely a burden off my shoulders. If I hadn't won with a six-shot lead it would have been pretty hard to take and pretty hard to come back from. But I was able to scrape in at the end. It's not about how many but how in the end. All these situations I have put myself in is all experience and I am gathering them all in. Obviously all the experiences I have had in the past helped me today and hopefully this experience will help me in the future."

The past had passed and Rory was now fully focused on moving forward to a brighter future.

****

On 1 March 2009, Rory McIlroy, fresh from his maiden European Tour victory, made his US Tour debut. In advance of the Masters, he had decided to play four events in the States as an ideal preparation for his first US major.

His first port of call was the Accenture World Match Play Championships in the Arizona desert. Before his first round clash with South African Louis Oosthuizen, Rory gave his views on his first World Golf Championship: "I'm coming in here with quite a good bit of form and it's great to be over here. It's nice to be able to play a schedule that consists of World Golf Championships and majors. I've had two good looks at the golf course now and it's nice."

He added: "It's interesting. The greens are still pretty tricky. It probably takes a little bit of time to get used to. But the course is in great shape and it looks like it's going to be a good week."

Now very much in the thick of it as one of the world's leading professionals, McIlroy was about to embark on a welcome break from the routine of tournament golf. And he had plenty of matchplay experience, as he revealed: "All the amateur golf I played growing up was matchplay. I played for Ireland in the European Championships and the home internationals. It's a game where most of our amateur events in Britain are matchplay as well, so it's a format we've grown up with.

"I think my game suits matchplay because I make quite a lot of birdies and I'll be able to throw in the odd double bogey here and there. We have grown up with matchplay and it's a great game as well.

I mean, it's head to head and that gets the juices flowing. So I'm really looking forward to it this week."

Rory beat Oosthuizen in his first match and then he faced another South African, Tim Clark, in his last 16 clash. After he had beaten Clark 4&3 to reach the quarter-finals, this is what Ernie Els said about him: "He's got a lot of confidence going now and obviously the win in Dubai was big for him. He got that little monkey off his back because he has been in contention quite a few times in the last six months. So he's comfortable now. He's hungry, as we say. So that is going to make him a major factor in world golf. I think you're probably looking at the next world number one as he's got all the tools."

McIlroy had actually gone four up after six holes in that match against Clark. The South African had beaten Tiger Woods 4&2, so his was an excellent scalp. After the win, McIlroy was gracious to his vanquished opponent, saying: "I think Tim didn't play his best golf. Understandably he was probably a little flat after all that happened yesterday and I came out and got off to quite a fast start and got an early lead, and I was able to hang on and get the win. It's great, fantastic."

Rory's prize for that win was a quarter-final clash with the winner in 2006 and runner-up in 2007, Geoff Ogilvy. He got off to a great start, birdying the second hole to go one up, but Ogilvy was soon back level. He won the fourth when his younger rival's putting let him down as he three-putted for bogey. Despite hitting a monster 388-yard drive on the fifth – the longest drive of the entire week – the momentum swung Ogilvy's way as McIlroy two-putted for bogey.

Rory clawed his way back again but, after finding the rough off the 11th tee, had to take a drop. He double-bogeyed and went one down again. He fell to two down at the 12th but reduced the deficit again at the 13th, to be just one behind. Then a real gunfight ensued.

An enthralling match saw the young Ulsterman do everything to try and rescue the situation as the holes began to run out. A brilliant birdie on the 16th was only enough to halve the hole but, one down with two to play, he still had a fighting chance.

Those watching were treated to superb golf from two players in the zone. In one corner you had an Australian former champion and runner-up and in the other, a real raw Ned Kelly with all guns blazing. Birdies, monster drives, brilliant pitching – he had it all. And the 17th was as good a hole as you will ever see in matchplay: a classic encounter between two gladiators giving their all with nothing between them.

First up for the galleries was Ogilvy, who was left with 200 yards to the green. His approach brought rapturous applause from the crowds as it finished just five paces from the hole. Having left himself with a putt from around 14 feet, it seemed like he had a glorious opportunity to win the match 2&1.

With an 8-iron, Rory went one better, leaving the spectators shaking their heads as he pitched to within ten feet of the hole. He had an even better opportunity to take the match down to the 18th. It would be a fitting climax to an epic duel.

The big Aussie was first up. If he missed, Rory had a chance to take it to the final hole. But Ogilvy sank it and ended up the victor.

But Rory could take great satisfaction from his week. Even greater consolation came from the fact that Ogilvy went on to win the title again.

For his second US event, and the first on the American circuit proper, Rory played in the Honda Classic a week later. He opened with a level par 70 and played steady golf over the next three days to finish -2 and tied 13th. His first Tour cheque amounted to $90,000.

The following week he played in the WGC Championship in Florida. At the halfway stage, Rory was bang there and in contention to win his first US title. Rounds of 68 and 66 left him three behind Phil Mickelson with Nick Watney a shot in front of him in second.

On so-called 'moving day', however, he could not get anything going and signed for a 72. He slipped further down the field with a final day 73 and in the end he had to settle for tied 20th.

Nevertheless, a top ten and two top 20 finishes in his first three US events was quite impressive from the youngster. And in his final warm-up event before the Masters, he made another top 20 when he tied 19th at the Shell Houston Open in Texas.

These positions were becoming the norm for Rory, as we again saw in his first ever Masters, when he tied 20th. To the American public, he was demonstrating class and star quality. In their eyes, he was a future winner in their own backyard.

McIlroy then flew back and forth between Europe and the US. He played two more events in the States beginning with the Heritage on April 16, where he failed to hit a sub-70 round. On +2, he finished outside the top 50. But even worse was to follow.

After taking a three-week break from golf, he set his sights on his first ever trip to Sawgrass. His performance there in the so-called fifth major, the Players Championship, turned into a nightmare.

Rory had no doubt watched from his armchair over the years, with much amusement like the rest of us, as great golfers found themselves in big trouble at Sawgrass. No hole better illustrates the treacherous conditions of the course than its infamous 17th.

Requiring no more than a wedge, this short par three still manages year after year to make fools out of the world's greatest golfers. The reason: from the tee, the green looks like a tiny target set as it is against the backdrop of water surrounding it on all sides.

It is a cruel hole. Each year as the 160 golfers begin their rounds here, almost every single one of them has the 17th on their minds. As they play through the preceding holes, they are all acutely aware of that bogey hole (pun intended) lying in wait up ahead. As they play their rounds, golfers can hear the roars, the screams, the shrieks and the 'oooohs and ahhhhs' of the crowds signalling that yet another ball has hit the water.

Then, when their own time has come to stand on that 17th tee, with spectators milling around and millions watching on TV, it can be like standing in front of a judge or executioner. The pressure can be enormous, and many limbs turn to jelly.

Here is another interesting take on Sawgrass and on Rory McIlroy, written by Jay Busbee, the American novelist, sportswriter, comic book writer and golf blogger. He wrote: "These kids today and their video games. So locked into their XBoxes and their Wiis and their Playstation 3s, they don't know what to do with life when it smacks 'em right in the face.

"Case in point: Rory McIlroy, who knows a thing or two about both real golf and the video kind. He kills time between tournaments by playing *Tiger Woods '09*, and just this week got his first live taste of

Sawgrass, a course he's completely mastered – he once shot a 54 over 18 virtual holes – on the game. Rory's verdict, according to Reuters:

"'It's a lot different. You get up to holes like 11 on the computer and you can drive it up to the big tree on the right, which is like 150 from the green. I had a good drive yesterday and was still hitting a five wood in. It is not quite like it is on the Playstation.

"'Yeah, I've found that hunting zombies and carjacking a Ferrari in South Beach is a lot tougher in real life than it is in video games, too.' (Tip: neither one is recommended.)

"Now, unlike the rest of us, McIlroy can actually play as himself in the game without having to create a slightly more muscular, slightly more handsome version of ourselves. Even so, no matter how graphically accurate the simulation may be, he's not even close to experiencing the real thing – not unless he's got a constant loop of goofballs yelling 'Get in the hole!' running on his iPod as he plays."

The 17th at Sawgrass is euphemistically known to many as the Island Green. Rory was about to get his very first taste of it and it would not be pleasant on his palate. He was not shown any mercy.

Even though he was two under par, he had really struggled through his round, which had included three bogeys. Then: splash! Rory took a triple-bogey six at the 137-yard beast.

Karl MacGinty of the *Irish Independent* described Rory's tee shot: "The Holywood youngster's jaw dropped in astonishment after his tee shot, hit with a wedge, flew right over the island green and disappeared into the dark green water. McIlroy turned and looked at his caddie, JP Fitzgerald, in disbelief. 'Did you ever see a wedge fly 150 yards?' he was still asking as he left the recorder's hut after signing for a first round 74."

This is what Rory felt about his first ever dice with the dreaded Sawgrass 17th: "It was 148 yards to the pin today. I hit a wedge and just flew the lot. I don't know if I got a gust or something. I wasn't going big with my third shot from the drop zone. I spun it back to the front and took three to get down.

"It's not a nice way to finish, but I didn't play that well today. I hung in well, though, and got it round. I thought getting it to two-under through 16 had been good for the way I was struggling a little out there. I battled well, but the way things happened through the last two holes undid all the good work.

"I'd struggled to find the fairways and you can't afford to do that around here, but I worked hard to make the up-and-downs. I thought I hit a perfect shot (on 17). It looked all over it, as if it was going to bounce maybe three or four yards from the pin and be close … but it just flew the whole lot."

Rory bogeyed 18 as well and his second round was even worse. Although he survived his second skirmish with the 17th, he had a day to forget. His first round 74 was followed by a 77, which included five bogeys and a double-bogey seven at the par five, 583 yard ninth.

After missing the cut at the Players, he returned to Europe, where he played several events leading up to his first US Open. He finished fifth at the BMW PGA Championship and 12th at the European Open.

McIlroy then played in his second major as a professional at the US Open. His final round of 68, two under par, helped him finish in a tie for tenth – his first top ten finish in a major. The following week, he finished 15th at the BMW International Open.

He then played in his second Open Championship, and his first as a pro, in July, finishing tied 47th. Later in the year, he finished tied third at the 2009 USPGA Championship despite rounds of 71, 73, 71 and 70 – his best result in a major prior to his US Open victory.

Banking €3.6 million in earnings, he ended 2009 ranked second in the Race to Dubai behind Lee Westwood, and in November he entered the top ten in the world rankings for the first time, at number nine. He was the youngest player since Sergio Garcia to be ranked in the top ten.

South African legend Gary Player praised Rory as the "most exciting young player in the world". And McIlroy returned the compliment by accepting an invitation from Player to participate in the 2009 Nedbank Golf Challenge.

It was held at the Gary Player Country Club at Sun City, South Africa in December. But Rory later withdrew from the event after feeling unwell. The jet-setting and the moving of mountains had taken its toll.

It had been a hell of a year and a 2009 that stamped 2008 into oblivion – 24 cuts made out of 25 on the European Tour was testament to that. Add to that his first win; three seconds; three thirds; a staggering fourteen top tens; plus over €3 million won. It was nothing less than phenomenal.

The cream was rising to the top at a fast rate of knots and it was very much "roll on 2010". The next big target of a major was within Rory's sights – not to mention the little matter of trying to crack America.

Chapter 8:
Sweet Home Carolina

The Abu Dhabi Championship was first on the agenda for Rory McIlroy in the new year. He made a pretty good start, too. Richard Bland, Keith Horne and Ian Poulter all shot opening 65s, with Rory one behind on -5.

On the second day his old Walker Cup comrade Shane Lowry shot up the European charts alongside Swede Peter Hanson with a 65 for a halfway total of -11. They lay a shot behind little-known Australian Rick Kulacz, who shot a best round of 63. Rory was next on 134 with Sergio Garcia and Martin Kaymer. But a third round 67 from Rory put him in ideal position going into the final round with Kaymer and Poulter.

The latter two shot 66s on the final day, with Rory narrowly losing out and Kaymer triumphing by a shot from Poulter. Rory, in turn, was two ahead of Lowry, who finished fourth.

Beginning with his USPGA third place finish back in August 2009, this result turned out to be McIlroy's eighth top ten finish in nine events on Tour. Nevertheless, he was thrilled with his seasonal bow as he told the press conference after his round. "It's a great way to start the season in the last group and going down the last just one behind and getting the juices flowing again," he reported. "It was a nice feeling and hopefully that will set the tone for the rest of the season."

Another top ten finish was secured a fortnight later when Rory tied sixth in the Dubai Desert Classic, three shots behind winner Miguel Angel Jimenez. The Spaniard beat Lee Westwood in a playoff after both players had finished on -11. McIlroy ended up eight under par and in truth he never really looked like winning. Two shots behind going into that final round on -9, his last round 73 ruined any chance he had. But he was still in very good form, as he had shown consistently the previous year.

As he took a break the following week to prepare for his second World Matchplay Championship in Arizona, there was every reason to believe that Rory might be on course to make a real impact in the majors. But before that, he had a score to settle.

When he lost to Geoff Ogilvy in that titanic duel at the WGC Matchplay event the previous year, it was generally expected that he could learn from that experience and be a future force in the event. After all, matchplay was his game and one that he grew up with.

Rory looked to be heading for a disastrous start to his World Matchplay week when he trailed American Kevin Na by four holes with just six played. But he snatched victory on the very last hole after a fantastic fight-back. He admitted to feeling huge relief: "I just hung in there and played good golf around the turn. I think I hit a really good drive on 15 which was important after missing the putt on the previous hole to get back to one down. When I went square through 16, I knew I was in pretty good position and I hung in well and had a great drive on the last, which put him under pressure. I was very fortunate to get through today and I'll need to play a lot better if I want to progress into the latter stages of the tournament."

Next up for McIlroy in the last 32 was England's Oliver Wilson. Rory's feeling that he was lucky to progress proved correct. He had struggled against Na, who was world ranked number 61, and he also struggled throughout against Wilson. The Englishman made the running for most of the match with Rory trying to play catch-up. Again, the Ulsterman fought back and he took the match to sudden death by having to hole a nine-foot putt on the very last hole – which he did.

On the second hole of their stalemate, the 20th, Rory drove into a bunker. Wilson replied with an immaculate chip close to the pin and it was all over for Rory. Wilson progressed to the last 16 while Rory stayed on in the States for a steady run of tournaments.

Carrying on from his previous struggles in the heat of the desert, his 2010 US Tour started pretty abysmally. Nothing went right for him in his first five events.

At the Honda Classic on March 4, opening rounds of 71, 69 and 75 meant that he was struggling way down the field. A final round of 69, one under par, meant he crept back up into the top 50, but he finished four over for the event.

Things didn't get any better at the WGC Championships in Doral the following week. A horrific opening 76 would in normal circumstances have seen him facing a quick flight home. He followed that with a 73 and two further 73s left him on +7 and way down in 65th position. It was the worst tournament he had played as a professional since the Bridgestone Invitational at the end of the previous season.

Back then, scores of 75, 70, 71 and 74 on a par 70 course left him trailing way down in 68th position on +10. In normal tournaments a golfer would not get to the point of running up such a score as the cut comes into play, but not in an invitational.

So the early signs in 2010 were worrying for Rory. He was struggling with his game, and it was about to get even worse. Not even a three-week break from the States could help him on his return.

When he missed consecutive cuts at the Shell Houston Open and the US Masters, for the first time he openly questioned whether he should play on the US Tour. To this day, he is undecided as to whether to play in Europe or the US. After that US Masters, it was back to the drawing board.

You knew things were serious when Rory again took three weeks away from America. It seemed as if he was slowly easing himself away from playing on the other side of the Atlantic. Family, friends and girlfriend Holly Sweeney were all no doubt coming into his mind and his golf was very definitely suffering. The evidence was there for all to see in his results.

A happy Rory in Europe was making eight top tens from his previous nine tournaments. An out-of-sorts, poor lonely boy was not very happy away from home. From his statements, Rory seemed to be coming around to the conclusion that he could do without all the hassle of playing in America.

The Firestone Country Club in Ohio; the Honda Classic in Florida; the WGC in Doral; the Shell Houston in Texas; and the Masters in Georgia are five really beautiful places. Try telling that to Rory McIlroy after five horrible results.

Strange faces, strange places, strange courses, strange accents and strange commentators were all weighed up in the 'pros and cons' game against his beloved Europe. It was a no-brainer. The scales were tilting heavily one way. Rory was all set to quit the States.

Next port in a storm for McIlroy was the Wells Fargo event at Quail Hollow in Charlotte, North Carolina. He must have felt like dumping his clubs and getting the hell out of there when he opened up with another very poor couple of rounds.

Scores of 72 and 73 had him on the verge of missing his third cut in a row. In fact, he was right on the cut line. One over par at the halfway stage showed that, mentally and physically, his golf game was still in the doldrums.

Shaking off all the shackles and all the shenanigans, he shot a six under par 66 in the third round to move to -5. Suddenly he was back in with a glimmer of hope. However, even stringing together good back-to-back rounds would probably only get him a top ten finish.

In the final round, a birdie on the fourth hole moved McIlroy to -6, and then he really set sail. A hat-trick of birdies on seven, eight and nine moved him up to nine under, and suddenly he was moving close to leader Phil Mickelson and getting in the mix.

From going nowhere in his opening two rounds, he suddenly found himself with a very real opportunity of winning his first title on the US Tour. The question was, could he keep this new-found purple patch going?

The par five tenth took the wind out of his sails. It was another glorious birdie opportunity but a par to Rory in that sort of form, and where he should really be looking at eagle or birdie, was akin to a bogey.

He made amends on the 11th. From the right side of the fairway, in the semi-rough, Rory played a peach of an iron. The ball landed 15 feet from the pin and rolled up to within a yard for yet another birdie. It was the shot of the day and it had the crowds whooping.

Glancing up at the leaderboard, Rory would have seen that it was now boiling down to a straight fight between him and Mickelson. Perhaps that realisation dawned on him. From a hopeless situation, suddenly there was real hope. Nerves came into play. He only made par at the next two.

Pull yourself together, Rory. Five holes left and it is between you and old Lefty. Finally, you have the chance to put things right. Five birdies already, and a glorious one at 11; you have the chance to put this away, bring home your first title from the States.

Birdie! The 14th hole gave Rory the outright lead at -11. The Yanks, loving an underdog, went wild with delight. The atmosphere they created was spurring Rory on, so much so that if the 11th was good, then the par five 15th was simply sublime.

A great drive came up to some 20 feet away from the water's edge. He played a full swing 5-iron which popped on to the green. Rolling straight for the pin, it came up just four feet short for an eagle chance! It was majestic and magic.

Rory's veins were pumping adrenalin. He was gritting his teeth and burning with determination. He now had that winning feeling. He was going to do it. Nobody was going to stop him now he could smell sweet victory in the air.

He demonstrated all that inward feeling after playing that terrific iron shot. When he saw where it landed, he turned round and flung his 5-iron 40 feet through the air to caddie JP Fitzgerald. Take that! There was no fist-pumping, no screams of "yesssss", just an inward resolve to finally get this job done. The weeks and months of turmoil could be erased from his memory over just a few more holes. He was tantalisingly close.

Tap-in eagle! The crowd hollered and rose in unison to applaud the young man, still not 21 years of age. Dressed in white trousers and a pale striped T-shirt with a white peaked cap, he looked like a majestic sailor striding aboard an awesome warship.

Rory was 13 under par and three shots clear of the field with just three holes remaining. You could hear the usual comments coming from observers: "It's his to lose," and "It's not over till the fat lady sings".

They were right. McIlroy found the fairway bunker on 16. But from the sand he played another unbelievable shot. His ball rolled up and landed just eight feet from the pin for yet another birdie. It was an incredible seventh, to go with that gem of an eagle.

It was just one of those days that you dream about before going out on the course. You dream the shots you want to make but it never turns out that way. Today, the 'zone' had arrived and Rory was riding the crest of it.

The par three penultimate hole was a dangerous, short test over water. Anything to the front was dicing with disaster, so Rory, quite rightly in the circumstances, played the percentages. His iron went to the safe side of the green at the back and left a long putt up to the hole for par. In a cosy position at -14 meant no heroics were required; just take the two putts. From 50 feet away, it rolled at the steady pace Rory imagined.

Then, as the ball climbed a little ridge in the centre of the green, it gathered speed as the contours now declined sharply towards the water a safe distance away. It gathered more and more speed. The green was like an Augusta ice rink.

There were shouts of "in the hole", and the ball was certainly obeying those instructions. It was heading straight into the heart of the cup. Rory watched intently with wide eyes and open mouth. For a few hundredths of a second, his ball fell ever so slightly into that white background but then, just as quickly, it came back up again and rolled on. It was a case of ecstasy and agony in equal measure in the same second. What an unbelievable near miss!

The importance of that putt lay in the fact that McIlroy was on the verge of shattering the course record. But at nine under for his round, he still had one more opportunity of breaking the record on the final hole.

But making a birdie on 18 would take some doing. It is a very dangerous hole as well as a long one. All along the right-hand side, leading up to and around the green, you have thick, leafy trees. To the left, there is a creek. Making that last hole even more treacherous is the very narrow entrance to the green, which slopes left. It is like a pass through a canyon. Go right and you could end up in trees; go left and you are most certainly in the water.

Rory threaded his ball through but ended up at the front part of the green, some 46 feet from the hole. He approached his potentially record-breaking putt. Head down, picking his line, he pulled back and released his putter with the same smoothness and authority he had shown all day.

The ball was visibly breaking in a slight arc from his right to left. As it neared the target, you could hear that familiar bass din from the swarms of onlookers all around the green. The noise level rose and rose until it exploded into one, unanimous, celebratory roar.

Rory McIlroy's ball swung straight into the cup. His ninth birdie of the day to go with his eagle meant he had finished with a -10 round. He had just shattered Quail Hollow's course record.

Sensational is the only word to describe his golf that day. It was simply out of this world. The gods had sent a message that they liked this young fellow. If we did not know that back then, we know now that they are on the right side of him.

Here was the evidence, on display before the world of golf, of the genius of this much talked about youngster from Northern Ireland. It was without doubt the greatest golf Rory had ever played as a professional, and he did it in front of watching millions on television.

It was not just his course record 62. It was every single facet of his game. Everything from his relaxed and easy-going, smiling demeanour to his ball striking came together on that memorable Sunday. Savouring every minute of his first US win, he said: "I suppose I just got in the zone. I didn't realise I was going eight, nine, ten under par. I just knew I'd got my nose in front, I was just trying to stay there.

"Ever since I was ten or 11 I wanted to be a professional golfer and you know it's been a crazy ride to this point. I'm just delighted to get here and get my first win of the year and to do it on a golf course like this is an amazing feeling.

"I'm going to have a bit of a party on Tuesday night down in

Sawgrass. If I was back home and had a win like this I'd be having a good one tonight."

Bob Harig, of ESPN, wrote an excellent piece after Rory's win during which he interviewed many golfers to get their feel on what the young man had just accomplished. He wrote: "This was a good day for golf – a very good day. It doesn't get much better than a guy who can't rent a car nor buy a drink in the United States shooting a course-record 62 alongside a greybeard of 24 to win his first PGA Tour event – or a teenager halfway around the world shooting 58 for that matter.

"Rory McIlroy has long been destined for greatness, a kid mature beyond his years already well-schooled in the rigours of the professional game.

"At 20, he has played in six major championships, and Sunday he became the youngest player since Tiger Woods in 1996 to win on the PGA Tour with a stunning victory at the Quail Hollow Championship."

Harig continued: "Rory McIlroy's stirring course-record 62 on Sunday at the Quail Hollow Championship helped the Northern Irishman win his first PGA Tour event. His ten-under-par effort came after learning that Japan's Ryo Ishikawa, 18, shot a 12 under par 58 to win a Japan Tour event by five strokes – his seventh title on the Japanese circuit."

McIlroy answered: "I'm just trying to keep up with him! I played that tournament [in Japan] a couple of years ago. The greens are so small, they can get the greens rock hard there. It's a very impressive round. Every time I've played with him, he's been great, and obviously with myself winning today as well, it looks good for the future."

Yes it does, and that is a very important point. Golf has long sought a few young players to step up and be the next generation of superstars.

McIlroy's caddie, JP Fitzgerald, a veteran who has worked for the likes of Ernie Els among others, cringed at the inevitable comparisons to Woods. But he did admit Sunday's win was special, saying: "The way he played the back nine was magic."

McIlroy had shot 30 over the closing nine at Quail Hollow to blow past the field and finish four strokes ahead of Mickelson. David Feherty, a CBS TV analyst and former European Tour player who is also from Northern Ireland, said: "I know I'm biased but was that as good as I think it was? He'll be a big star as long as he wants.

"He could have birdied the last three. You're supposed to soil yourself on the last three here. Especially when you're 20. The hairs on my body are still standing up. It's astonishing to have the guts, the courage to do it. When I was that age, I was thinking, 'How am I going to lose this thing?' He was going further and further and further ahead. And that does remind you of somebody."

The reference, of course, was to Tiger Woods, who has made a habit over the years of stepping on necks and not letting up on his way to victory. McIlroy did the same that Sunday.

"He's got a lot of talent, there's no doubt about it, and he had a great day out there," said Anthony Kim, who played with McIlroy that Sunday. "That'll help his confidence. He's been having a tough year out here and now he'll be ranked in the top ten in the world. He can play out here."

It was funny for Kim to refer to McIlroy as a kid. Kim, a three-time winner on the PGA Tour, is all of 24. When he played at the Masters with McIlroy and Ishikawa he said: "That's when I really felt old."

"He's a young player, but he's got the game of a veteran," said Mickelson, who had been grouped with McIlroy for two rounds earlier at Doral. "This guy has got all the shots."

And to think, just a few weeks before, McIlroy was questioning his decision to join the PGA Tour and attempt to play both in the States and in Europe. He was considering passing on Quail Hollow and the following week's Players Championship, having missed three straight cuts.

Padraig Harrington noted the pressure McIlroy was feeling because "at home, no matter how he does, the focus is on him".

"I got home, took a few days off and said there's no point in feeling sorry for yourself," said McIlory, who had played a couple of practice rounds the previous week at two of Northern Ireland's finest and most famous courses, Royal County Down and Royal Portrush. Feeling better about himself, he was still not putting up the numbers. But on Friday, he had come to the par five seventh hole, his 16th, two shots off the cut line – and made eagle.

"Most important shot of the year, to be honest," he said. "If I don't make eagle there, I'm practising at Ponte Vedra this weekend (for the Players Championship). That could have been the turning point of my season."

As an example of how popular McIlroy is, players including Jim Furyk, Aaron Baddeley, Lee Westwood and Harrington waited around to offer their congratulations.

It didn't hurt that he ended the round in style with a birdie that left the ground shaking. "I suppose to cap a day off like that was probably fitting, to hole a putt like that on the last," McIlroy said. "It's one of those moments that you'll always remember. When it went in, I couldn't believe it."

If you can get a chance to obtain a video of Rory's final round, grab it, or go online to view it. Watch his ball connection – from his driving to his pitching and putting. Never mind his half-swings; concentrate on his full swings with the driver and irons. Awesome! There is no other word to describe them.

Then have a good look at his putting. The way he reads them and lines them up, his posture, his poise, his beautiful strokes are all masterly. Text manuals can be ripped up; just copy Rory's Quail Hollow 62!

It was the greatest golf he had ever shown to the expectant world. Even taking into account what he would go on to achieve the following year, and his US Open win, that one still remains the greatest round of golf that Rory has played in his career to date.

Harig referred to Japan's Ryo Ishikawa and his 58 across the Pacific. Lest it be forgotten, Rory missed opportunities when he only made par at two par five holes – the fifth and the tenth. His ball also popped into the hole and out again on the 17th.

It was no surprise in the circumstances that he missed the cut in the Players Championship at Sawgrass less than a week later. The euphoria of his first win, the brief celebrations and thoughts of getting home for bigger and better celebrations took their toll.

But then it was back to normality and, when the curtains began to close on another golf season, it ended for Rory as it had begun: more questions in his mind about home and where he feels comfortable and where he is happiest.

North Carolina would forever more find a very special niche in McIlroy's heart. But before that, and after it, in Shanghai at the HSBC in November, once again Rory intimated that he was quitting the US Tour.

Then, exactly a month after his mutterings of discontent, he finished fourth at the Chevron World Challenge in Sherwood Country Club, California, four shots behind his great friend Graeme McDowell, who beat Tiger Woods in a playoff.

In the eyes of the entire golfing world, the boy wonder had the future of all futures at his feet. But home is most definitely where the heart is. Rory was unhappy, and he would continue to feel unhappy.

Chapter 9:
Root of the Problem

If there is one major besides the US Open that Rory McIlroy seems destined to win, it is the USPGA. Even before the 2011 event at the Atlanta Athletic Club course, he stated in a press conference that his game was made for this particular tournament.

In his two previous attempts at the USPGA, Rory had actually been in with a great chance of winning it. His debut at Hazeltine Golf Club, Minnesota in 2009 saw near-record crowds turn up to watch the 91st running of what is traditionally the season-ending major.

Tiger Woods opened up with a -5, 67 in the first round to lead by one shot from Padraig Harrington. Rory shot a 71, one under par, and he was quite content with his first performance in the event, particularly since Hazeltine is a tough course.

But a round of +1, 73 the following day left him well off the pace as Woods increased his lead at the top to seven under. Another round of 71 on the third day put Rory back into under-par figures for the tournament, and he was not out of it.

He shot another nice round on the final day. But a two under par 70 was never going to trouble Tiger or YE Yang, and Rory finished his first USPGA at -3, in a tie for third place with Lee Westwood.

Woods, who led going into the final round and seemed sure to add yet another major to his haul, buckled under the pressure of Yang's dogged persistence. The Korean matched him shot for shot and eventually won by three shots at -8.

Yang became the first Asian to win the USPGA, but it was a case of what might have been for another Irishman. Behind Woods going into that final round, Harrington actually started the day level with Yang. However, when he looks back on the event he will wish to forget in a hurry the horror that befell him on a fairly easy par three. Padraig blew his chances of winning a fourth major by running up a quintuple-bogey eight on that hole.

Rory admitted to showing very poor judgement on the greens. He started with a double-bogey but then hit a rich vein of form, rattling in four birdies. But another bogey on the 12th, and some missed opportunities, put paid to his chance of victory. Nevertheless, it was his highest finish in a major to date, and he summed up: "I've had some good results lately and I'm looking to build on these results next year and hopefully try to do a bit better. I think, coming into this week, I didn't have my best form or my best game with me. So to finish tied third is a great result for me."

On to 2010 at Whistling Straits, and Rory came even closer to winning the USPGA. He did indeed build on his impressive debut of the previous year and by the time he left Whistling Straits, he could only think of how close he had come to victory.

In a similar way to Hazeltine the previous year, he opened with a pretty ordinary 71, but he followed that with a -4, 68 in the second round to lie on five under at the halfway mark. It was a case of two cuts made from two in the PGA.

Matt Kuchar, on -8, led by a shot from Nick Watney, so Rory was in a nice position with two days to go. Watney had other ideas. On 'moving day', he put space between himself and the rest of the field by shooting a magnificent 66 to go to -13.

Not to be outdone, and keeping himself very much in the hunt, Rory shot 67 and was only three shots back on -10. He was level with Dustin Johnson and both were to play in the second last pairing on the final day.

Alas, for the second year running, things just did not swing Rory's way. Although he got the better of Watney, who fell apart with a final round 81, Bubba Watson shot a 68 to join Martin Kaymer in a playoff at -11.

Agonisingly, Rory had finished just a single shot adrift. Although he had tied third yet again, it was hard for him to stomach the fact that he had failed to break par in the last round. Had he managed to do so, he would have gone close to winning. He said: "I'm OK. I had a few bad swings the first few holes and I managed to recover well. After those escapes, I had a few chances that went by on the back nine.

"It was just one of those days when I felt I hit good putts but nothing went in. I'm pleased overall as I played nicely all week and I just needed to find one more shot in there on any of the four days, which is disappointing."

Clearly saddened and somewhat deflated by his near miss, he did however feel a great sense of achievement at putting himself into position to win. He was also very happy at the way he hung in there, as he added: "I was very proud at how I ground it out. It wasn't the start that I would have wanted. I made a great up-and-down at the first hole and another great up-and-down at the third, and I held it together on the front nine."

There was, however, a worry concerning something else Rory said. In the light of what would eventually happen to him in the last round at the Masters, it was significant that he admitted to feeling the heat as he went out for the final round: "It was my first time being in contention in the last round of a major and in the second last group. I was feeling it on the first tee and it was a new experience for me. Hopefully it will stand me in good stead for the future."

Having tied third in his first two USPGAs, one could see why Rory now fancied himself to win it in future. He said as much before the 2011 event, but the drama that was to unfold there was something that no one, least of all Rory, could have seen coming.

****

Despite the fact that he played with good friend Darren Clarke, it is best not to mention the 2011 USPGA to Rory. Going into the event he was confident and full of hope after two previous third placings. Very quickly, it turned into an event full of controversy.

On the third hole, Rory hit his tee shot into the semi-rough. But unknown to him, to the TV crews and to the watching millions, an amazing thing then happened – a small boy walked over to the ball and picked it up. Before Rory arrived on the scene, the child's parents told the toddler to put it back where he had found it. The drama was only beginning. The young child placed the ball at the foot of a tree.

Although it was in a very tricky position nestled directly behind the tree, Rory saw no cause for alarm. Like almost every golfer on the planet – amateur or professional – who has at some stage encountered this scenario, he knew he had a few options. Normally it boils down to two – have a good firm go at the ball or take the safe choice and play it out gently on to the fairway. Rory, after surveying the ball and feeling it was sitting up nicely, decided to have a go.

He gave the ball a good strong strike and it ricocheted up into the air and came to rest just a few feet away, with his club flying through the air. The airborne club was actually part of the plan, as he explained later: "It was dangerous. I thought if I could make contact with the ball and just let the club go, I might get away with it. It was a shot that I felt like, if I took it on and pulled it off, it could have saved me a shot."

Rory was grasping his wrist in pain, however, and it soon became clear that something bad had happened. Just underneath the ball, invisible to the eye, was the root of the tree. Any gardener will testify that it must have been like striking hard rock.

Rory immediately called for ice, and he was given the option of a ten-minute time-out, which he refused. Returning to his ball, which was now a little way back from the tree, he decided this time to hit out and put bend on the ball. And he played it very well, leaving an up-and-down for bogey. Furthermore, and after his second shot from behind the tree, there seemed to be no adverse effect from the injury, and he carried on with an ice pack wrapped around his wrist and forearm.

A discussion with officials about getting his club repaired, revealed that he was almost certainly going to complete his round. But there was more cause for worry as the follow-through from his tee shot on the fourth hole left him wincing in pain.

But again Rory soldiered on, so much so that the crowd warmed to him on the fifth as he chatted with Clarke. Grimacing again after his tee shot there, the crowd shouted "hang in there, Rory," to which he replied several times, "thank you".

It was noticeable that he had no strength in his right hand because of the pain in his arm. When bending down to stick his tee in the ground he was wincing and had to put the tee into his left hand to carry out the operation. But through all his trials and tribulations, his talent and genius were about to shine through once more. He splashed out of a bunker to within a foot for a tap-in birdie and made it consecutive birdies on the sixth.

Comparisons were now beginning to be made with Tiger Woods, who famously won one of his many majors on one leg. The golf media were quickly latching on to the fact that Rory had gone from one over par to one under on one arm!

And so his dramatic day continued with bogeys and birdies, and a physio accompanied Rory for a few holes before deeming him fit to conclude his round. He ended with a level par 70 – a fantastic effort in the circumstances.

Rory was seemingly OK to continue his USPGA but reflecting on his opening round, and particularly that third hole, he admitted: "It was a mistake in judgment."

After entering the Atlanta Athletic Club clubhouse for a few minutes, he brought out some extra wet towels from the locker room. He then got into the back seat of his courtesy car, driven by friend and associate Stuart Cage, and it was off to see the doctor.

An MRI scan late on Thursday night showed no long-term damage. In fact, there was not so much as a tear. A strained tendon in his right wrist was diagnosed and, to great applause, Rory appeared on the first tee on the Friday morning. Before starting, he said: "If it wasn't a major, I probably would have stopped yesterday. To be honest, looking at the scans, they said, 'Look, you can't do any more damage to it, it's up to yourself. If you want to play and you feel as though you can play

OK and carry on, then do. And if not, then you shouldn't play.' I feel as if I can play, so the decision was purely up to me."

With his wrist heavily strapped and a new 7-iron from Titleist to replace the one that had been broken in the battle with the root, Rory went out and shot a three over par 73.

All things considered, and with so many big names missing the cut, he did well to make the weekend and chalk up three out of three cuts made in the USPGA. Even then, he was not at all happy – but it had nothing to do with his wrist and everything to do with the 17th hole in his second round.

On the 16th, he swung in a fantastic birdie from nearly 50 feet to get to -1 for the tournament. The crowds went wild, yelling out his name as he headed to the 207-yard par three over water. With his new 7-iron in hand approaching the tee, he changed his mind and switched to a 6-iron.

As Rory watched the shot anxiously in mid-air, he seemed to have hit it a bit higher than he wanted. He was shocked when it came down short of the green and, glancing over at caddie JP Fitzgerald, he muttered inquisitively: "Wet?" Worse was to follow as he three-putted for a triple bogey, killing off all his momentum.

His 2011 USPGA ended there and then. Although he soldiered on for the last two rounds, his play degenerated. But not before more debates had raged and questions had been asked about Fitzgerald.

JP had been the subject of a huge controversy at the Irish Open when a sort of *ménage a trois* developed involving him, Rory and US golf journalist Jay Townsend. That will be dealt with in more detail in the next chapter. This time Townsend remained silent on the issue, but there were plenty of others to take up the gauntlet.

The incident on the 17th where Rory changed his mind over choice of clubs and looked at JP was not the main issue. Instead, golf pundits were baffled as to why Rory had chosen to play that shot behind the tree on the third hole. Reporters fired questions at him about his decision. Although he had already answered it by stating what his intentions were, he also had to defend JP once again by coming out with statements like "he's not my father".

But after he had admitted that it was a "misjudgement", experienced observers were still baffled. How, they asked, could a caddie stand over a professional taking such a shot? Some even compared JP and Rory to Tiger and Steve Williams.

It seems an absolute certainty that, with the wolves smelling blood, the 'JP controversy' is set to run for a long time to come. How Rory keeps them at bay will be interesting to watch. Like Townsend, on this issue, he bit his lip and stayed silent.

****

Another 'Irishman' actually won that 2011 USPGA, and in the process he also won his first major. Keegan Bradley was a most unlikely winner of the event; he and the rest of the field looked to be playing second fiddle to Jason Dufner.

Dufner, who had failed to win on the US Tour in his seven years of playing it, was out on his own. With just four holes left in his round he led by five shots and his first win looked assured. His first success was also set to become his first major win. But in events even worse than McIlroy's Masters debacle – when the young Rory had a full round in front of him – the experienced Dufner suffered an amazing collapse. In sight of the chequered flag, he threw it all away.

Bradley looked to have blown his chances when he triple-bogeyed the par three 15th. However, he showed steely resolve to birdie both 16 and 17 brilliantly, to go into a three-hole play-off with Dufner. Indeed, when the crowd burst into their Olympic-like chant of 'USA, USA, USA' to signal the fact that America were about to end their majors drought, it seemed to give Dufner even more of the wobbles while inspiring Bradley.

As the playoff ended and Bradley threw his arms in the air to celebrate victory, little did he know that he had just etched himself into history as the first golfer to win a major with a long putter. His victory also put him in line for US Player of the Year after his victory at the Byron Nelson Classic earlier in the year.

Everything had finally fallen into place after years of struggling, as the 25-year-old admitted afterwards: "When I was 12 I did a bit of skiing. I was competing in a slalom in Killington. I remember sitting on the top of that hill. It was raining, cold, sleeting and I remember thinking to myself: 'I love golf so much more'. But this is unbelievable because two and a half years ago, I was on the Hooters Tour grinding for survival."

Thirteen years later, and with millions watching him worldwide, his Irish roots were about to come out. In fact, it turned out that he was more Irish than many Irish in America – perhaps even as Irish as many in Ireland! His aunt, Pat Bradley, explained: "We're an Irish family and we have that Irish toughness. He showed some real Bradley toughness out there and I'm just so very proud of Keegan in the way that he fought back and brought it home. He has also honoured his father, who is a club professional in Wyoming."

Six times a major winner in ladies' golf, Pat is a member of World Golf's Hall of Fame. Her grandparents hail from Ballycotton in Cork and she herself is an honorary member of Old Head and Kenmare golf clubs. Not only that, Keegan's father Mark was a regular competitor on the US Tour, so he was certainly bred for the job. But he also had special words for his aunt afterwards as he held the Wanamaker Trophy as USPGA champion, saying: "I grew up going to her tournaments as a kid. I remember watching her and literally staring into her face. But she was so into it that she didn't even recognise me. But I totally idolised her."

Typically of Ireland, everyone was claiming to be related to him! In fact, long after Irish players Harrington, McDowell and McIlroy had fallen out of contention for the title, Irish TV back home was trumping up the chances of 'Irishman' Bradley. Expressing his own thoughts on the matter, he said: "My family is intensely Irish. I'm very proud of my heritage and I even have a shamrock logo on my golf bag. I was over there when I was eight and I really want to go back again so bad. I want to play in the Irish Open, I really do."

After a statement like that, there is no doubt an invitation will now go out year after year to Keegan; no doubting either that some of his five uncles will turn up to see him: Corkmen Chris, John and Tom Bradley compete each year in Kenmare's 'Three Brothers Championship'.

Rory McIlroy can only hope that he will be the next Irishman to win the USPGA. After playing in it three times, his game does indeed seem made for it. But he will forever want to forget the root of a tree on three.

Chapter 10:
The Controversies

A book chronicling Rory McIlroy's career would not be seen to be doing the subject justice if it did not refer to controversies involving the young golfer. Although many may not wish to see them referred to again, for the purpose of fairness and balance they simply have to be.

There are a few smaller controversies that will be dealt with briefly towards the end of this chapter, but as Charlie Mulqueen of *The Examiner* has pointed out, there are also a couple of major ones.

By far and away the biggest controversy of Rory's career so far is one that is set to be played out for many decades to come. It is the question of his, shall we say, patriotic allegiance. Mulqueen provides the intro: "There have been times when I wished Rory McIlroy had taken time to formulate an answer before expressing a view on anything that might be regarded as controversial.

"The remark, for instance, that he 'looked forward to being a member of Team UK' after it was announced that golf would be part of the Olympic Games rankled with many – and not just those with nationalistic leanings or the members of the GUI who had helped him along the way in his amateur days."

In the *Telegraph* of 29 September 2009, Mark Reason tried to make sense of it all: "If you are McIlroy or Tommy Bowe and golf and rugby union are accepted into the 2016 Olympics at next week's vote of the International Olympic Committee, do you represent Great Britain or Ireland?

"McIlroy told *Telegraph Sport*: 'I'd probably play for Great Britain. I have a British passport. It's a bit of an awkward question still. It would be huge to play in an Olympics. I'd love to get an Olympic gold medal one day.'"

It is strange that golf and rugby should have been up for Olympic inclusion at the same time – both will have places in the 2016 Games – because these are the sports that have historically unified Ireland. Ulster's rugby team come under the governance of the Irish Rugby Football Union and players from the north and the south turn out for one Ireland team.

Golfers do the same. Formed in 1891, the Golfing Union of Ireland is the oldest golf union in the world and the presidency rotates between the four provinces. It does not matter if you hit your wedges in Ulster or Munster, you play amateur golf for Ireland.

Professional golf also recognises one Ireland. At November's World Cup in China there will not be a team from Northern Ireland and a team from the Republic; there will just be a team from Ireland. In 2011 McIlroy and Graeme McDowell, both Ulster lads, play for Ireland. In 2009 it was McDowell and Paul McGinley, who is from the south. On many previous occasions it has been McGinley and Padraig Harrington.

McDowell said after the International Olympic Commitee's executive board proposed golf and rugby should be included in 2016: "It's a strange one. Golf's an all-Ireland sport. I'd play for anyone. I've never been able to explain why golf's an all-Ireland sport and rugby's an all-Ireland sport but soccer is two different teams. It'd be an honour to represent your country and I don't mind which one I play for."

He added: "It's the biggest sporting event on the planet. I'd love to be involved in it, love to win a gold medal. It's every young man's dream, huge for golf around the world. Golf needs to go to the masses. I'm not a fan of golf being an elitist sport. Fingers crossed I get a chance to do it."

Harrington said: "In a country like Ireland, becoming an Olympic athlete is setting yourself apart. It is a major deal in Ireland. To be an athlete is an honour in itself."

But Harrington will not have to make a choice when golf makes it to the Olympics. McDowell and McIlroy, like many athletes from Northern Ireland before them, will have to declare an allegiance.

A few years ago, Eddie Irvine got into an undeserved bit of bother over what flag to hoist when he finished second in a Formula One race. Captain Peter McEvoy had a similar quandary at golf's 2001 Walker Cup. Someone had to hoist the tricolour at the opening ceremony but the two Irishmen in McEvoy's team, McDowell and Michael Hoey, were both from the north.

McEvoy said: "In the end it didn't prove a problem and Michael was happy to do it as the amateur champion, but it could have been. It is strange that something like the Olympics comes along under the banner of good and we are now faced with this potential problem. It feels a bit of a retrograde step."

Peter Dawson, the chief executive of golf's governing body, the R&A, said: "It's a question that has yet to be resolved, but I suspect that giving the players the choice is the likely outcome.

"Perhaps that can change in the future. Perhaps young men and women will not have to make such an invidious choice. Perhaps golf and rugby's inclusion in the Olympics can provide a bridge to unite Ireland across all sports."

Let us not forget Barry McGuigan, one of Ireland's all-time great sports stars. The boxer swept Ireland off its feet back in the mid-80s and early 90s despite the fact that he had similar but seemingly bigger controversies in his life than Rory. McGuigan, from Clones, County Monaghan, married a Protestant girl and he had to take out British citizenship in order to pave the way for him to fight for the British featherweight title in his quest for the world title. This, at the height of the Troubles, did not stop him enjoying the adoration of an entire island.

Indeed, as a young boy, I wrote to Barry at his home in Clones to ask for his autograph. What I received in reply was unbelievable. He sent back a black and white photo of himself training on the heavy bag in his amateur days in his Clones club. Along with them were two signed photos of him wearing the British feathwerwight title belt. He also invited me to Clones!

McIlroy, like McGuigan, is a Catholic. He grew up in a Protestant suburb of Belfast. He went to Sullivan Upper in Holywood, which is a non-denominational school, and he has never uttered a word about, or shown an interest in, religion or politics.

This was a stance also taken by McGuigan who, incidentally, is a good friend of Rory's who attended the 2011 British Open, where he followed McIlroy around the course during the first round.

So why should anyone make demands to know where Rory's allegiances – if any – are? He and his family have quite rightly stayed silent on the subject. It is the right course of action to take when one considers what has gone on in Ireland in the past.

Carl O'Malley, in a piece on the *Irish Times* website of 20 June 2011, summed it up: BRITISH? IRISH? DOES IT REALLY MATTER?

"'Why are you celebrating a British golfer?' The above was one of the texts received by *Newstalk* this morning as they discussed the stunning display produced by Rory McIlroy in the US Open at Congressional at the weekend.

"As his final round unfolded towards victory, families across the island and the world gathered to savour a remarkable achievement for a 22-year-old golfer from Holywood, County Down.

"A young man, who with every cheeky smirk and grateful wave of acknowledgement to the crowd, epitomised what it is to be a champion – brilliant but humble and ruthless but sportsman-like.

"His embrace with his father Gerry was a truly special moment, the culmination of a shared journey, during which there must have been a multitude of emotions – stony silences, tearful reconciliations, slammed doors and high fives.

"Most of us took our little piece, because ultimately that's why we watch, so we can share the tiniest morsel of excellence that we will never experience.

"Then, on Monday morning, as we strut to the bus stop like Wee-Mac coming down the 18th, some gobshite dumps all over it by texting a snide question that doesn't matter.

"There are three ways of looking at it, as far as I can see:

"**1. Rory McIlroy is British.** If it suits you, he holds a British passport and has said he would like to represent Britain in the 2016 Olympics. And who has any right to argue with that?

"**2. Rory McIlroy is Irish**. If you'd prefer, he can be seen as a product of Irish golf, having travelled the world as an amateur under the umbrella of the Golfing Union of Ireland and represented the island of Ireland (all 32 counties) at the highest level.

"**3. Rory McIlroy is Rory McIlroy.** He belongs to himself, his parents, his true friends and Holywood Golf Club. He's a sportsman. He entertains. He captivates. He amazes. He makes people happy."

****

The second of the main controversies involving Rory happened at the Irish Open following his opening round in Killarney on 28 July 2011. After his US Open victory and Darren Clarke's Open Championship win, the crowds flocked to Kerry to give both their support.

At the start, they had plenty to shout about as Rory hit the ground running. He carried out one of his incendiary blitzkriegs as he was -4 through the front nine. But then things started to unravel – on and off the course.

On the tenth hole, he hit his ball into the left rough behind a big oak tree. He then recovered magnificently with a high lob over the tree to within 12 feet of the pin for a par save.

Commentator Jay Townsend described it as a miracle shot and one of the best he had seen. However, all that was to change over the next few holes and by the end of his round, a controversy had blown up that ran for weeks and weeks.

On the 18th, McIlroy found a bunker. He took out a long iron and made an attempt to find the green, which was guarded by a lake. Instead, he found the water and ended up with a double-bogey six. From being -4 at one time, he finished with a 70 for -2.

As his ball splashed into the water, to groans from the huge galleries, Townsend said: "You see. That's what happens when you try to find the green with that sort of shot from the bunker. That's silly."

A little while after his round, a war of words erupted between the American commentator and McIlroy. Initially, the Irish television channel RTE thought the row was to do with Townsend's 18th hole remarks. But the story went a lot deeper than that.

Most people know by now that Rory McIlroy uses the social networking site Twitter. He especially likes to 'Tweet' with his good friend and fellow Northern Ireland golfer Graeme McDowell. Later, as he relaxed, Rory wrote the following on his Twitter page: "RORY McILROY @McIlroyRory Belfast, Belfast GB Had a great dinner with my parents … It's time for some table tennis! I need to stop my losing streak!

"Just did a Q&A with Graeme McDowell at the Irish Open. Was great fun with a few interesting questions from some curious fans. lol (laughs out loud)

"Well I stand by my caddie," (in response to a Tweet from Jay Townsend).

"Shut up … you're a commentator and a failed golfer. Your opinion means nothing," (in further response to Tweets from Townsend).

It transpired that when McIlroy Tweeted to Townsend that he was "standing by his caddie" and that Townsend's "opinion meant nothing", he was directly responding to some stinging criticism from Townsend. Earlier, the Florida-based pundit had stated: "(that is) some of the worst course management I have ever seen beyond U-10 boys' golf … because JP allowed some shocking course management today." Townsend also suggested that McIlroy should hire Tiger Woods' former caddie, Steve Williams.

On the face of it, it seemed brazen and brave of Townsend to take the bull by the horns. However, it later became clear, through a statement from McIlroy, that Townsend had been having a swipe at caddie JP Fitzgerald for three years.

Referring to an event in Switzerland some years earlier, Rory said: "He's been having a go at JP every now and then since then and this was the first time that I've responded – it was the straw that broke the camel's back – but now I've blocked him on Twitter so I won't be reading anything any more."

Rory, in subsequent comments on the matter, stated that JP had taken him to the verge of Masters glory and also to a US Open victory, so he must have been doing something right.

Townsend, who played on the European Tour from 1991 to 1998, never won a title. His CV lists 13 top ten finishes, with the highlight being a third place finish in the 1993 Heineken Open in Spain (later the Catalan Open). Now, as a golf commentator, he considers himself fortunate to be getting paid handsomely for something he loves.

Before the 2010 Ryder Cup at Celtic Manor, he told BBC viewers: "I used to play golf for a living and now I get to travel the world and report on the best golfers on the planet. On top of that, I get paid to do it. OK, now pinch me to let me know that this is real!"

A few days after the JP incident, Townsend attempted to put it to bed. He referred to it as being an "unfortunate" episode and, as far as he was concerned, it was over. However, Rory was unrepentant and stood by everything he said. Asked if he had any regrets, he said: "No, not at all. He doesn't need to be that opinionated. I don't really have any respect for the man after what he did or after what he's done the last three years."

Quoted by Fergus O'Shea in the *Irish Sun*, Rory added: "JP is one of my closest friends. I've had to deal with it for three years and not really said anything. But he's just kept at him and at him, so I had to say something. I don't care if he criticises me, I can take the criticism. JP can't stand up for himself.

"It started in Switzerland back in 2008 and it was just one comment too far. JP has taken me from 200th in the world to major champion and fourth in the world."

As I'm about to quote two more people who give their own raw and forthright views on the subject, it would be unfair of me, as the author of this biography, to sit on the fence and not give my own opinions.

Putting myself up, therefore, as my own judge and jury, I would ultimately clear Rory; I would find in favour of Rory McIlroy. That said, on one of the charges I would find him guilty.

Rory told us that Townsend had been having a go at JP for some period of time. I watched and listened to Townsend's commentary on Rory and JP at that Irish Open and there is no doubt that the evidence is there to point this out.

Other remarks that Jay has made have to taken into consideration. Without quoting him fully, there is another moment in his commentary where he laughs and, in a patronising tone, criticises the golf media in this part of the world ("I just don't get you guys.")

Personally, I feel it is a golf commentator's or writer's prerogative to report and ask questions but not to go to such lengths as to confront a player on social networking sites, or anywhere else, on a particular view – a view you are trying to force on that player. That is very wrong.

It is also wrong to keep trying to enforce your viewpoint over a period of time. Townsend may not believe that JP is giving Rory the kind of advice and leadership that a caddie of the undoubted quality of Steve Williams would. However, McIlroy is the one calling the shots, and they are working for him. In all probability, it is therefore a pointless exercise on the part of Townsend, or any pundit for that matter, to try to get or influence someone to change.

Rory is not entirely blameless. He is guilty of calling Townsend "a failed golfer". Taking into account the camaraderie of Tour golf, and sport's so-called dressing-room *omerta*, he was wrong. In time, Rory may see that he should not have insulted Jay with such a remark. He need only place himself in Jay's position to realise that.

For example, if Rory, God forbid, were never to win another major, and if 30 years from now a golfer was quoted as calling Rory McIlroy a "failed one-hit-wonder", that would be very hurtful to him.

When asked about the subject, 2011 British Open winner Darren Clarke said: "Everybody is entitled to their opinion. JP Fitzgerald is one of the best caddies that I have ever had on my bag and I respect Jay as a commentator as well."

In summation of the row – which, in a similar way to the Mick McCarthy v Roy Keane 2002 football World Cup row, had many entering the For and Against camps – here are the two opinions I referred to earlier that hold their own very strong case points.

In Ireland's *Evening Herald* of July 29, Ian Mallon, who followed Rory and JP around the course as part of the media cortege, courageously wrote: "Only time will tell why Rory McIlroy chose the Irish Open to shed his impish innocence and morph into the grotesque snarling spectre which we all feared was coming.

"OK, so he's not the truculent, belligerent Scotsman-with-a-sore-head that Colin Montgomerie became … after all, he's got caddie JP Fitzgerald for all that.

"But something is up with Rory. I walked around with him yesterday as did Jay Townsend, the respected golf commentator whom McIlroy berated from the cold comfort of his BlackBerry last night.

"Townsend's crime? For pointing out the glaringly obvious: that Rory's course management was not up to scratch. Rory's 'shut up, you're a failed golfer' retort was both shocking and extreme.

"Townsend, whom I admire on BBC Radio 5 Live, missed the point about Rory. It's not that Rory's course management was particularly bad, it was that his overall attitude was terrible.

"For much of yesterday, Rory did not want to be there or, as a fellow seasoned hack said: 'he'd prefer to be in the scratcher (bed) with [tennis player] Caroline Wozniacki!

"If Rory was the picture of peeved off, then his caddie JP was a thoroughly miserable individual. Steve Williams, Tiger Woods' sacked bagman, was always arrogance personified. But unlike JP, Williams always spoke respectfully to the crowds in a way that was firm but polite.

"JP, on the other hand, took continuous potshots at the wonderfully behaved galleries in Killarney if someone had the audacity to finger a camera or phone when Rory was not addressing the ball. As Rory trudged around like a schoolboy being led through the school gates by an overbearing parent, it was apparent that all is not well in Rory's world.

"Darren Clarke on the first tee wore a grin as wide as the lake and Padraig Harrington, for all his woes, was his usual terrific self despite possessing a game that appears to be deteriorating beyond repair. But as it will be for years to come, it was all about Rory. It's just a pity that he chose Ireland to announce his coming of age."

Charlie Mulqueen of *The Examiner*, a long-serving and well-respected Irish golf scribe and radio reporter, and a man with whom Rory would have had a long association through his amateur years, wrote: "Now we have the rumpus about the Twitter spat between Rory McIlroy and the American television commentator Jay Townsend. I must admit that telling Townsend to 'shut up' and describing him as 'a failed golfer' was unworthy of the fourth best golfer on the planet.

"However, who gave Townsend, whose only claim to fame on the golf course was to finish runner-up in the Catalan Open in 1993, the right to state that McIlroy had been guilty of 'some of the worst course management I have seen beyond U10 boys' golf competition?'

"The tone of the comment surely indicates that Townsend has a bee in his bonnet regarding McIlroy and his caddie JP Fitzgerald. That agenda was referred to by McIlroy, who described this latest incident as 'the straw that broke the camel's back'. It first became apparent after Rory's meltdown in the Masters, where Townsend was openly critical of Fitzgerald, and was followed on Thursday by another uppercut that 'JP allowed some shocking course management today'.

"Furthermore, he would have been better advised to praise McIlroy for the magnificent manner in which he accepted the mortification of that hugely publicised collapse. It was a massive ask of any 22-year-old, but Rory held his head high as he bounced off the 18th green and courageously turned to face the media.

"It reminded me of a similar development after he followed up his opening round of 63 in last year's British Open with an 80 in dreadful conditions the next day. Many presumed he would slip quietly away, but again he faced the reporters and microphones. Fast forward to this year's US Open, where McIlroy turned in an astonishing performance to claim the title by eight shots. The man on the bag again was a certain JP Fitzgerald.

"Where was Jay Townsend then? Where was the eulogy to this remarkable young man who clearly connected comfortably with the man by his side?

"I have one or two questions for Jay Townsend and the others who would have a go at Rory McIlroy. What were you like when you were 22? Did you ever say or do something in the heat of the moment that you quickly regretted?

"Rory, my advice to you in future is to treat these people with the contempt of your silence – and to stick loyally by JP Fitzgerald – and whoever may succeed him in time – by repeating the words of Thursday night: 'I stand by my caddie.'"

The controversy concerning Rory's caddie came up again at the USPGA, the final major of 2011. The trials and tribulations of the events surrounding Rory's injured arm have been covered in the previous chapter. But there were many who questioned JP Fitzgerald for allowing Rory to take such an audacious shot in the first place. There were also several other shots in that round that golf pundits questioned – but this time Jay Townsend remained silent.

There have been other controversies in Rory's career, though on a much smaller scale. Rory's complaint about the weather during the Open Championship was one, but there was also the questioning of all the time he was taking off Tour, away from golf.

Following his US Masters debacle, Rory took well over a month off. In some newspapers he was pictured in a bar with his head back, looking a little worse for wear and swilling from a bottle of Jägermeister.

Probably having a pop at Rory, Phil Mickelson criticised golfers for taking such time off. Lefty was making a point that all golfers have a responsibility to their profession as well as to sponsors and the public. They are also in a very lucky and privileged position.

Rory responded to criticism by saying that he is a professional golfer and that he will decide when and where he plays. He ended by saying that he was thinking of getting another bottle of Jägermeister!

When Rory did not attend the 2011 Scottish Open at its new home of Castle Stuart, just a week in advance of the Open at Sandwich, Mickelson again had an apparent swipe at those who did not turn up when he said: "I feel that the winner of next week's British Open will come from among those who are participating here this week."

On the eve of the Open at Royal St George's, Mickelson also told the BBC: "I'll be playing week in and week out right through until the end of September."

In a show of support for Rory, and others who like to take a break from the hectic Tour, Padraig Harrington said in an interview some weeks later that looking back on his career now, he had one big regret – that he had played far too much golf.

Late into the season – and in the year that golf legend Seve Ballesteros passed away – Rory also caused controversy by announcing that he would not participate in the Vivendi Trophy (Seve Trophy) as he was taking a couple of weeks off.

The vast majority of golfers do not, and have not, taken the amount of time away from the game that Rory has. But as he has stated, that is his choice. Perhaps it will become a new trend, and it will certainly help to stave off 'burn-out', if nothing else.

But as Charlie Mulqueen intimated, all these controversies would simply not have surfaced if Rory had chosen to do a Björn Borg and stay silent. As the Shakespeare quote goes: "give every man thine ear but few thy voice".

Perhaps Rory will do well to heed that advice from now on and let his magnificent golf do his talking. The bottom line is this: he simply does not have to make a comment on anything that will blow up in the news from the moment he utters it.

Chapter 11:
Fame, Fortune and Future

Rory McIlroy has established himself as one of the world's biggest sports stars. He is a household name and he is right up there standing toe to toe with Tiger Woods as one of the most recognisable players – and one of the first mentioned – in the world of golf.

It has taken him a relatively short space of time to achieve this. He first came to real prominence in 2004 in Ireland when he started to take the country's top amateur events by storm, breaking many records in the process.

Great Britain sat up and took notice in 2007, when he played in the Open Championship as an amateur and Jeremy Chapman proclaimed for all to hear: 'The boy who will one day be king'. He opened up with the third best round of the day.

He cemented his growing reputation there in 2010 when he took St Andrews apart. Equalling the Open record for the lowest round of 63, he played with such ease and near perfection that he could easily have taken the outright record with 62.

America and the rest of the golfing world were taken by storm at Quail Hollow and in 2011 at the Masters and US Open. As he made the rest of the field look second class in those events, the world's print and broadcast media fell over themselves to headline him.

Taking a four-shot lead into the final round, he kept the headline writers even busier by creating huge drama with his last round collapse. The euphemism 'Rory's Masters meltdown' was created.

All around the globe, even those outside golf and sport suddenly felt sorry for him, and they took the boyish-looking Rory to their hearts – even more so when golfing great Jack Nicklaus took Rory to one side to give him help and advice.

Armed with all the goodwill shown towards him, Rory dusted himself down and came back stronger just a few weeks later, so much so that he absolutely trounced the entire field in the US Open to win his first major.

The scenes around the 18th green at Congressional, where he hugged his father Gerry, wishing him 'Happy Father's day', could have taken place in a soppy soap opera. One could picture hordes of people watching their televisions and sobbing into their tissues.

This was all helping the rapid rise of Rory's star, which burned even brighter following his first major win when he began a sort of 'celebrity celebration' tour. He was about to embark on a merry-go-round of meetings with some of the world's most famous people. It started in his hotel the next morning; it continued on Chubby Chandler's private jet on the way home; and his rubbing shoulders with the rich and famous has continued ever since on an almost weekly basis.

Darren Clarke was one of the first to text him a message of congratulation in the early hours of the morning after his US Open triumph. Because of his hectic schedule, he even turned down an appearance on the David Letterman Show in the US.

A quick stop-off in London enabled him to meet up briefly with golfer Lee Westwood, as well as British TV entertainers Ant and Dec. When he arrived home to his sprawling mansion outside Holywood, a letter from British prime minister David Cameron awaited. Other politicians he would meet on his hectic travels were Northern Ireland first minister Peter Robinson as well as deputy first minister Martin McGuinness. Everywhere he went. fans screamed and sought his autograph.

While being driven to a homecoming celebration at his beloved

Holywood, Rory revealed some of his A-list celebrity friends who had been texting him messages of delight all day and the previous day on the private jet. As he listed the names, there was a sparkle in his eyes. He felt an immense pride in himself at being the centre of attention among such illustrious names. It was almost as if he was still a young boy worshipping some of his heroes as he said: "It's great getting messages of support and congratulations from so many people, and from friends and family, but to get them here on my phone from people like Wayne Rooney, Rio Ferdinand, Alex Ferguson, Rafa Nadal, Jack Nicklaus and Andy Murray is just so fantastic."

He would not have to wait long before thanking his good friend Rafa in person. On Tuesday, June 28, Rory flew to London to watch the tennis star get in some practice on an outside court at Wimbledon ahead of his quarter-final that day. Rory was in for a huge surprise as he got an even bigger bonus – he also met tennis legend and fellow 'Irishman' John McEnroe, as well as Britain's number one player Andy Murray. On his meeting with the popular Murray, he said: "I'm a big tennis fan even though at home I got rid of my tennis court and changed it into a five-a-side soccer pitch! I grew up watching Tim Henman here at Wimbledon and now we're all behind Andy Murray. Hopefully, he can win his first grand slam."

From his seat in the royal box, McIlroy looked resplendent in a dark suit, white shirt and pink tie. But it was just possible to notice a few dark bags under his eyes – no surprise after a hectic weekend schedule of US Open parties at home.

One party was described as 'wild' and among the invited guests at that gathering were English boy band JLS, good friends of Rory's. One of his best friends from Holywood, Harry Diamond, had also organised a party for him in a trendy bar the previous week.

When Nadal reached the Wimbledon final, on Sunday, July 3, Rory was back in the royal box again. He had been flown over the previous day in a private jet laid on by *Sky Sports* television. And that gave him the opportunity to see another one of his pals perform on that Saturday night. Rory had prized ringside seats to see David Haye fight Vladimir Klitschko for the world heavyweight boxing title.

He was in a Peter Pan dream world as he Tweeted: "All packed for the weekend. World heavyweight title fight followed by Wimbledon final! Carlsbergdontdoweekends!" And he added to his great golfing friend Graeme McDowell: "In the royal box on Sunday. I can't wait."

It was easy to see why. Joining 22-year-old Rory in the hot seats were Formula 1 racing driver Jenson Button and his stunning girlfriend, Jessica Michibata. Also there was Prince Harry.

Haye was comprehensively outpointed by the giant Russian, who retained his world title, and Nadal was swept aside by Serbian Novak Djokovic in the Wimbledon men's final. But Rory was a winner everywhere and his beaming smile would not leave his face.

Rory's love life was also constantly in the newspapers. In particular, the on-off relationship with his long-term girlfriend Holly Sweeney was a source of continual fascination for the tabloids. Being so young, and being together for such a relatively long period, they were really childhood sweethearts. The pair had met in August 2005 when Rory was 16 years old and Holly 14.

In a BBC Northern Ireland documentary entitled 'Rory – major breakthrough', filmed just after Rory won the US Open, Holly recalled the day when she first laid eyes on Rory: "I was up at the golf course caddying with a couple of the girls and he was practising. He came over and said hello and that's how it all started. I didn't even know who he was at that stage. He is still the same guy. Not one thing about him has changed.

"Being a champion does not come into it. You have to keep him grounded and say and do the same things you always do – like going to the cinema or going to Tesco."

After almost five and a half years together, the couple split up in December 2010. As his star continued on an upward curve, Rory was becoming more and more in demand at golf venues around the world, which meant long periods away from home. He acknowledged: "At the start of a new year in 2011, I wanted to focus totally on my game and just take a break or whatever."

From Holly's point of view, the feeling was mutual. Studying sports technology at the University of Ulster, she explained: "It was always going to be tough to take a break from each other. But in the end, we both decided to do our own thing. I needed to step it up with uni (university) and he needed to do his own thing with golf."

However, when Rory experienced his last round collapse at Augusta four months later, one of the people there to console him was Holly. This forced him to have a rethink and they reunited, as he explained: "It was nice to see her at Augusta when my management company flew her over. I gave her a big hug and said something like I was sorry she wasted her time in coming. But having her there made that Sunday night a lot easier, having someone there you really know.

"I realised pretty quickly that I made a mistake. I had to do a lot of begging and grovelling to get her back! She is fantastic. She definitely keeps my feet on the ground. She knows me better than anyone else and she knows the things to say to me."

There is little doubt that their reunion had such a positive effect on Rory's mind that it inspired him to his runaway first major win. As he arrived home at his €2.5 million mansion, Holly came down the stairs to another huge embrace – and the gleaming US Open trophy.

On Piers Morgan's US chat show Piers Tonight, Rory had never seemed happier, saying: "She's still going to university trying to get her degree and I'm out playing golf, but we see a lot of each other as we live together. There's no wedding bells at the minute. Holly needs to finish school and get a degree. She's the brains of the couple!"

He added: "We know it's never going to be normal. We're going to get a lot of attention – good and bad – but it's something we're going to have to learn to deal with."

Then came a huge shock. On Monday, 18 July 2011, Rory's management team released to the world a rather vague press anouncement that said the couple had split. It began: "Rory McIlroy's relationship with Holly Sweeney came to an amicable end before the British Open Championship."

To escape the intense media speculation and tabloid headlines such as 'Rory's love match as Holly flees', Holly went on holiday to Jumeirah in Dubai with a friend. The headline proclaimed that Rory was having an affair with female tennis star Caroline Wozniacki. This had come to light when a member of the public posted on the internet a video of Rory and Caroline having dinner together in a restaurant.

At the time Rory remained tight-lipped and refused to comment on the stories, which gathered pace rapidly over the next few weeks and months. From her side, Holly also stayed silent, preferring to Tweet a picture of herself enjoying a beautiful Jumeirah beach.

After disappointing at the USPGA due to an injured wrist, Rory immediately flew to Cincinatti to watch Caroline play in a tournament. It was probably the first real indication that things were becoming fairly serious between them.

The *Irish Independent* front page of Tuesday, August 16 carried a Associated Press picture of Caroline and Rory sitting together and looking very happy by the side of a practice court. Rory was holding a bottle of Evian water in one hand and a mobile phone in the other. He was crouching and listening to Caroline who, dressed in white tennis gear, was looking down lovingly at him.

Ten days later, an almost identical picture in the British tabloid the *Daily Mirror* showed Rory and Caroline at a tournament in New Haven, Connecticut. This time Caroline was dressed in a black evening three-quarter length dress, carrying a bottle of Evian and with Rory looking lovingly into her eyes.

Earlier, Rory had sat with Caroline's father Piotr in the stands and together they had cheered Caroline on. She won and reached the semi-finals of the event. Later they enjoyed an evening stroll with tournament director Anne Worcester – and the world's press.

It was a significant moment because on that day, August 26, Rory finally told the world that the Danish tennis player was his new girlfriend. Adding that it would be "pretty cool" if she could win the US Open the following week, he said: "Why it's going so well is that we have so much in common. Obviously we're in different sports but we're pretty much in the same position at a young age and we can talk about things that probably a lot of 21-, 22-year-olds can't talk about. It's nice to have someone that sort of understands what you're going through."

The weeks of speculation had ended. Also ending were the salacious and scandalous stories that had sprung up. Some, including one which will be dealt with in a following page, were trash, only serving to show Rory the kind of gutter treatment he will face in the future.

****

At this moment, according to the *Sunday Times* Rich List 2011, Rory McIlroy has a net worth of £7 million sterling. This represents a £2 million increase on the previous year.

That figure is only an estimate. In truth he is worth an awful lot more than that. The fact is that Rory and some of the world's other top golfers, like Phil Mickelson, could earn much more than that amount in just one season on Tour.

In an extremely good year, with several wins and perhaps a couple of majors in the bag, Rory's net worth could be £14m. That is not counting the huge amount of money he could earn from the multi-million dollar endorsements that may come his way.

So that *Sunday Times* figure is a little misleading. To date, Rory has amassed just under €10 million in prize monies won on the European and US golf tours. But it must also be remembered that his professional career is only in its infancy, having begun in 2007.

In 2010, he also earned £1.7 million from various advertising and sponsorship deals. This is where Rory will really earn his corn. No amount of money won in golf can ever match the sort of cash Rory can earn off-course without even working hard.

Not so long ago, there were newspaper reports that were touting Tiger Woods as the first sportsman in history on the verge of becoming a billionaire. It may at first seem total gobbledygook, but there is probably a certain truth in it. Though Woods is probably not now going to break through that barrier as he is no longer the huge marketing force that he once was, it seems certain someone else will take up the billionaire mantle.

In American basketball, some players are earning colossal amounts of money, while how do you put a price on the world's greatest footballer, Lionel Messi? He is priceless. If Barcelona were to put him on the market now, the bidding would start at £200m.

Rory McIlroy is one of the hottest young sports properties in the world today. If he continues to perform in the majors as he has in 2011, the money will be falling at his feet like confetti.

Chubby Chandler signed McIlroy to his team several years ago and he must be beside himself with the prospect of what can be achieved.

He has laid on everything for Rory in the last four years and already the trappings of wealth are beginning to show. A beautiful, €2.5 million mansion in the hills of Holywood, County Down comes with an in-built gym and surrounding lands that include a purpose-built practice golf course and tennis court – which has been converted into a five-a-side football pitch.

It has even been reported that Rory is looking to buy a property in Florida as he prepares to play more tournaments on the US Tour in 2012. But one report that did the rounds, concerning Rory's purchase of a car for $2 million, was shown to be false.

Among other cars, McIlroy drives an Audi Q7, but not the Bugatti Veyron that several papers proclaimed he had purchased in 2011. The world's most expensive sports car was not on his shopping list, as he told Ryan Tubridy on Ireland's The Late Late Show.

Appearing on the longest-running chat show in the world on March 18, he said: "The great thing about Twitter is that you can shoot stories like that down straight away. I don't think I'm anywhere near the stage yet of splashing that amount of money out on cars."

Tubridy then asked Rory: "Are you comfortable with the press attention as your star ascends higher?" After pausing for a few seconds, Rory answered: "Yes. I think I'm going to have to be able to deal with it for the majority of my career. There are times when you don't like it and you would rather be anonymous, but I suppose that if people want to know more about you, then you must be doing the right things."

That was a show that celebrated everything that is good in Irish sport, coming as it did on the weekend of St Patrick's Day. But no amount of accepting press intrusion, or what the papers publish, could prepare Rory for a story that followed four months later.

Writing in the Irish *Daily Mirror* on Saturday, 23 July 2011, under the banner headline: IT'S GAME, SET & MATCH FOR MCILROY; RORY LOSES OUT IN GAME OF LOVE, Paul Martin wrote the following: "They say behind every great man is a greater woman. In showbiz, behind every greater woman is usually a Prize A idiot. And this week, folks, that idiot is our own golfing hero Rory McIlroy.

"In the time-honoured tradition of men that have it all, he bit the hand that fed him. We've seen this siren go off countless times before. The classy girlfriend ditched as soon as a little success and a short skirt passes by.

"This was far from a gentlemanly break-up, folks. Despite the tears, I bet Holly would love to shake the passer-by's hand that took the grainy footage of Rory and tennis star Caroline Wozniacki cosying up over dinner and drinks as she dutifully stood by him at home.

"Holly stood by Rory for six years when nobody knew his golf handicap, let alone his name. For heaven's sake, she even turned a blind eye to the nerdy freckles and ridiculous poodle style hair.

"So Rory, remember all the hard times when Holly stood by you. The tears at Augusta, the years of being a golf widow while you toiled in the bunkers at the back of your plush house and the countless days standing in cold and rain as you carved out your dreams.

"Like all these men who think the grass is always greener on the other fairway, Rory will learn the hard way that the burger never tastes as good as the steak. Here's to Holly – a classy birdie even when Rory's pursuing a bit of rough."

'Widow'? I would say Martin got carried away there as it is generally accepted that, at such an age as Rory's, we are all exploring the world, and that we break hearts and have our hearts broken. They were not married. Rory is 22 and Holly only 20! They both have the right to go out, meet people and have fun.

So to write something like that is grossly irresponsible. It is also highly dangerous and there must come a time when the law comes into play and makes it a criminal offence to write such things. An unfair and misleading article can inflame hatred towards people like Rory, and it can also put a person's life, or the lives of their families, in danger. You do not need to go back too far to see what has befallen certain sports, film and rock stars to realise that.

The only person at liberty to talk about this subject in such a serious, direct and forthright way is Holly Sweeney. The fact is, she is the only person who knows Rory in that light. She is the only person who knows the full truth regarding their split.

When you take that into account, you realise how callous and careless that article was. Furthermore, at an age when people are only discovering themselves, were Rory and Holly not already preparing to split when they took a break prior to that pathetic piece? Did Holly not announce publicly that Rory had golf to concentrate on and she had uni?

This is precisely the sort of thing that countless millions of young people go through. No surprise, then, that reports say their split was amicable and they remain friends.

As regards Caroline Wozniacki, she is reputed to be one of the fairer ladies on the tennis circuit. Always good humoured and smiling, she is supposed to be a very nice girl who hails from a very respectable family. Someone should send her that so-called article.

After all, it is only fair that she be alerted to someone trying to score an unfair point as her back was turned. More to the point, her good reputation has been tainted and sullied in public by Paul Martin.

Rory is no doubt able to look after himself and he has already hinted that a lot of this is water off a duck's back to him. He will certainly need to be thick-skinned because on October 1, Martin was at it again. Under a photograph of Rory and Caroline kissing at an American football night, Martin wrote in his *Mirror* column: "It's enough to make you puke. Curly-haired lothario Rory McIlroy and his tennis ace girlfriend Caroline Wozniacki checked into the Tacky Towers this week. Rory had your columnist reaching for the sick bucket when he presented the female tennis No 1 with her own personalised golf club – with the sickly inscription 'Wozzilroy'.

"PM [the name of the column is Paul Martin] is reliably tipped off that Rory needs to break out a few new tricks for his latest romance. I'm told he gave the exact same gift, a few years back, to a certain Ms Holly Sweeney.

"Hopefully Wozniacki won't find out Rory's got a bit of history in the golf club present stakes or she might, ahem, 'serve' him with his marching orders."

****

Rory McIlroy has repaid Chubby Chandler in kind by giving him a US Open and a near miss in the Masters. As his stock market price soars, so his marketability becomes limitless. The world of golf is now firmly at his feet.

But in a dog-eat-dog world, there is a price to be paid. Rory must keep winning. In particular, he has to go to the next level and win another major. In fact, like all the greats – Woods, Ballesteros, Nicklaus, Player, Watson and so on – he must win several majors. The road to the future is paved with gold but, as Rory has already acknowledged, it is success on the course, and particularly the winning of many more majors, that is important.

Padraig Harrington believes he can do it: "If you are going to talk about someone challenging Jack Nicklaus's record haul of 18 majors, then Rory is your man. Winning majors at 22 with his talent – he should have 20 more years in him, meaning maybe another 100 more majors where he could be competitive."

After a chance meeting in a Florida shopping mall, the great Jack Nicklaus himself has taken an almost fatherly interest in Rory. The pair have met and talked at length on many occasions. Following one exchange between the two, Rory revealed: "Jack told me that there's going to be pressure from everyone else, so I've got to make sure in the future that I really want it. So he stressed that I've got to go out there always expecting to play well and to put pressure on myself to play well."

That advice from Nicklaus came in advance of the US Open – and Rory went out there and controlled that event from start to finish. He won easily and that is the sort of play and mental attitude that he will need to keep to rigorously for many years ahead.

Talent is not enough. Rory must work hard. Above all, he must practise hard. He must put in endless hours of practice in order to perfect certain aspects of his game. That is the message coming from those in the know and those who have been there and done it.

Practice makes perfect and there are no doubt aspects of Rory's game that he must improve on. Some have already questioned whether or not he has the game to win Britain's Open Championship – and one man who played him in a final reckons that he knows the reason why.

Eddie McCormack has always maintained, even before the so-called golf experts pointed it out, that Rory will struggle to win the Open unless he changes one particular facet of his game, as he explained: "Far be it for me to give Rory advice as he is obviously doing so much right over the last few years. But if I was to pinpoint one criticism of his game, I would say that he hits the ball far too high.

"It is all very well doing that on a lot of golf courses – particularly inland. But I do feel that is the reason why he has struggled in the British Open. Because of that, he will find it very hard to string four good rounds together in the Open.

"In the British Open, as well as in other events like the Irish Open, if he continues to hit the ball so high, it will mean that the ball will be carried by the wind and blown off course from its intended target.

"So in that aspect of his play, I think he'll have to learn to adapt to the conditions. If he can fade it, or hit the ball lower, which I'm sure is no problem to him, then he can definitely win an Open."

Rory is already looking forward to next year's first major, the Masters. It was one of the first things on his mind when he injured his wrist at the USPGA, and he is itching to get back to Augusta and to correct the last round mistakes of 2011.

Between now and then, Rory will be very much in demand – on and off the course. Already the recipient of Golfer of the Month and Shot of the Month awards, he is now in line for a couple of much bigger awards. Golfer of the Year is definitely one, although he may face stiff competition from Luke Donald and Keegan Bradley. He is also a firm favourite for one of the world's most prestigious and sought-after sports awards – the BBC Sports Personality of the Year.

On the course, though, is where it ultimately matters and if Rory is looking for some sound advice for the future, he need look no further than at the very beginning of this book. In the foreword, the legendary Gary Player had a hidden message for Rory.

It had to do with complacency. One of the reasons that Tiger Woods has won so many tournaments and majors was because he has, or had, the 'fear factor'. Many observers firmly believe that when Tiger's competitors saw him climbing the leaderboard, they froze. They knew that Tiger would fight tooth and nail to grab a tournament by the neck and make it his. His competitors had no stomach for the fight – a fight they believed they would lose.

Rory must learn to do the same. He must build a steely determination to win, such as the one he displayed at the US Open. Even when that event was won, he still turned on the style and was full of concentration. His adrenalin was running and he was very much in the zone.

Woods brought this fighting attitude into all events – those on Tour as well as the majors. Rory will probably be very disappointed with himself that he did not grab the chance of winning two events in a row after he returned from injuring his wrist at the USPGA.

The European Masters in Switzerland and the Dutch Open, both in September, were events that were there for the taking. He finished third in both but he let many chancest slip away. Those events were great opportunities for Rory to instill fear in his opponents. When he plays the same guys again, will they feel he is going to take the event and throttle it, or bottle it?

Rory did show some mettle and resolve in the Alfred Dunhill Links Championship in Scotland at the beginning of October. Two brilliant rounds at his beloved St Andrews (-7 through the front nine on the final day!) enabled him to grab the runners-up cheque of over €350,000, behind countryman Michael Hoey.

Gary Player's words ring so true. There have been so many golfers who failed to fulfil their potential. Countless numbers of multiple winners and major winners became content and satisfied with their lot and never went on to build on success.

The consistent big cheques that rolled in for finishing runner-up or in the top ten became their ultimate goal. The once-steely attitude turned to "why do I have to work hard and practise hard when I can make easy money as often as I want?"

But the story of Rory remains an inspiration to people everywhere. He is a credit to his beautiful, hard-working family and to his country. His is the true meaning of a rags to riches story. Above all, he is a role model for young boys and girls all over the world.

Rory, you were given a gift by the golfing gods and we will all watch in the hope of seeing you become one of the greatest golfers of all time. But remember, time waits for no man.

Tomorrow, as sure as Tiger was sent yesterday and you are here today, there will be another golf whizz-kid given to the world. So listen to the words and advice Gary Player has given you: "Rory, you are now faced with figuring out how to balance your needs amidst constant media coverage and celebrity. Most importantly, you must find out how to avoid complacency and settling for winning only once in a while.

"Rory, YOU have the game, now go out and show yourself and the world that YOU have the desire. Remember, the harder you practise, the luckier you get."

Rory's Vital Statistics

First major win and his record-breaking four rounds

US Open 2011, Congresssional

Round 1																			
Hole	01	02	03	04	05	06	07	08	09	10	11	12	13	14	15	16	17	18	
Par	4	3	4	4	4	5	3	4	5	3	4	4	3	4	4	5	4	4	
Score	3	3	4	3	4	4	3	4	5	3	4	3	3	4	4	5	3	3	= 65 (-6)
Round 2																			
Score	4	3	4	3	4	4	3	2	5	3	4	4	3	3	4	4	3	6	= 66 (-5)
Round 3																			
Score	4	3	4	4	3	5	3	4	4	4	3	4	3	3	4	5	4	4	= 68 (-3)
Round 4																			
Score	3	3	4	3	4	5	3	4	5	2	4	5	3	4	4	4	5	4	= 69 (-2)
																	Total		268 (-16)

British Open record-equalling round

British Open 2010, St Andrews

Round 1																			
Hole	01	02	03	04	05	06	07	08	09	10	11	12	13	14	15	16	17	18	
Par	4	4	4	4	5	4	4	3	4	4	3	4	4	5	4	4	4	4	
Score	4	4	3	4	5	4	4	3	2	3	2	3	4	4	3	4	4	3	= 63 (-9)

First US Tour win and course record

Wells Fargo 2010, Quail Hollow

Round 4																			
Hole	01	02	03	04	05	06	07	08	09	10	11	12	13	14	15	16	17	18	
Par	4	3	4	4	5	3	5	4	4	5	4	4	3	4	5	4	3	4	
Score	4	3	4	3	5	3	4	3	3	5	3	4	3	3	3	3	3	3	= 62 (-10)

First European Tour win

Dubai Desert Classic 2009, Dubai

Round 1																			
Hole	01	02	03	04	05	06	07	08	09	10	11	12	13	14	15	16	17	18	
Par	4	4	5	3	4	4	3	4	4	5	3	4	5	4	3	4	4	5	
Score	4	4	4	3	3	4	2	4	3	4	2	4	6	3	2	4	3	5	= 64 (-8)

Rory's 'Masters meltdown', Augusta, 2011

Round 1																			
Hole	01	02	03	04	05	06	07	08	09	10	11	12	13	14	15	16	17	18	
Par	4	5	4	3	4	3	4	5	4	4	4	3	5	4	5	3	4	4	
Score	4	4	3	2	4	3	4	5	3	4	3	3	5	3	4	3	4	4	= 65 (-7
Round 2																			
Score	4	4	4	3	3	3	4	5	3	4	4	4	4	4	5	3	4	4	= 69 (-3
Round 3																			
Score	4	5	4	2	5	3	4	5	4	5	4	3	4	4	4	3	3	4	= 70 (-2
Round 4																			
Score	5	5	4	3	5	3	3	5	4	7	5	5	5	4	6	3	4	4	= 80 (+8
																	Total		284 (-4)

Rory's 'majors' record to date

Year	'07	'08	'09	'10	'11
Masters	N/A	N/A	T20	M/C	T15
US Open	N/A	N/A	T10	M/C	WON
The Open	42	N/A	T47	T3	T25
USPGA	N/A	N/A	T3	T3	64

Total	Wins	2nds	3rds	Top 10	Top 25	Top 50	Other	MCs
13	1	-	3	1	3	2	1 (Injury)	2

Rory's World Golf Championships/World Matchplay record

Year	Played	1st	2nd	3rd	Top 10	Other	Prize Money
2009	6	nil	nil	nil	3	3	€889,000
2010	5	nil	nil	nil	3	2	€976,000
2011	*3	nil	nil	nil	2	1	€312,000

Rory's Professional European Tour record

(excludes US Majors/WGCs/Matchplay)

Year	2007	2008	2009	2010	2011
Starts/Cuts	4/4 (100%)	28/17 (60%)	17/16 (94%)	9/9 (100%)	8/8 (100%)
1st	nil	nil	1	nil	nil
2nd	nil	1	2	nil	1
3rd	1	nil	2	2	3
Top 10	1	5	3	4	1
Top 25	nil	4	2	nil	2
Top 50	1	6	5	2	1
Other	1	1	1	1	nil
Missed Cuts	nil	11	1	nil	nil

* (2011 dated to end-September)

Rory's Professional US Tour record

(excludes British Open/WGCs/Matchplay)

Year	2007	2008	2009	2010	2011
Starts/Cuts	0/0	0/0	8/7 (88%)	12/8 (67%)	6/5 (83%)
1st	N/A	N/A	nil	1	1
2nd	N/A	N/A	nil	nil	nil
3rd	N/A	N/A	1	1	nil
Top 10	N/A	N/A	2	2	1
Top 25	N/A	N/A	3	nil	1
Top 50	N/A	N/A	nil	4	nil
Other	N/A	N/A	1	1	2
Missed Cuts	N/A	N/A	1	4	1

* (2011 dated to end-September)

Year	2007	2008	2009	2010	2011
World Rank	95	36	2	13	*3

Rory's estimated earnings from WGCs/Europe/US

Year	Amount	Biggest Cheque
2007	€227,000	3rd Dunhill Links - €211,000
2008	€695,000	2nd European Masters - €222,000
2009	€3,164,000	3rd Dubai World Chmps - €324,000
2010	€3,306,000	1st Wells Fargo - €859,000
2011	€2,296,000	1st US Open - €1,003,000
Total	€9,738,000	

Rory's Ireland Internationals & Inter-Provincial Amateur Record

BOYS INTER-PROVINCIAL MATCHES 2003 – 2004

Played	Won	Drew	Lost
11	6	2	3

BOYS INTERNATIONAL MATCHES 2003 – 2004

Played	Won	Drew	Lost
12	7	1	4

YOUTHS INTER-PROVINCIAL MATCHES 2005 – 2006

Played	Won	Drew	Lost
10	5	3	2

YOUTHS INTERNATIONAL MATCHES 2005 – 2006

Played	Won	Drew	Lost
4	3	0	1

SENIOR INTERNATIONAL MATCHES 2005 – 2006

Played	Won	Drew	Lost
12	6	3	3

	Played	Won	Drew	Lost
Total	49	27	9	13

POINTS WON: 31.5 from 49

Rory's Ryder Cup record

2010 Celtic Manor, Wales – Debut for Europe

Session 1 Fourballs: R McIlroy & G McDowell v S Cink & M Kuchar – Halved

Session 2 Foursome: R McIlroy & G McDowell v S Cink & M Kuchar – Lost 1up

Session 3 Foursome: R McIlroy & G McDowell v Z Johnson & H Mahan – Won 3+1

Session 4 Singles: R McIlroy v S Cink – Halved

Overall match result – Won (1 win from 1 played)

Rory's Ryder cup points – Won 2pts from 4

Overall team points – Europe 14 ½ USA 13 ½

Rory's Vivendi Cup (Seve Trophy) record

2011 – Withdrew

2009 Paris, France – debut for GB & Ireland

Session 1 Fourballs: R McIlroy & G McDowell v S Kjelsden & A Quiros – Won 4+3

Session 2 Fourballs: R McIlroy & G McDowell v F Molinari & A Hansen – Lost 3+1

Session 3 Greensomes: R McIlroy & G McDowell v H Stenson & P Hanson – Won 2+1

Session 4 Foursomes: R McIlroy & G Mcdowell v S Hansen & S Kjelsden –Won 2+1

Session 5 Singles: R McIlroy v H Stenson – Won 1up

Overall match result – Won (1 win from 1 played)

Rory's Vivendi Cup points – Won 4 pts from 5

Overall team points – GB & Ireland 16 ½ Continental Europe 11 ½

Rory's stature

Height – 5' 8"
Weight – 11st 7lb

Clubs in Rory's bag

Driver: Titleist 910 D2, Shaft: Rombax 7V05 Loft: 8.5

Fairway Woods: Titleist 909 F2 13.5°, 906 F2 18°

Irons 3 - 9: Titleist 710 MB Forged

Wedges: Titleist Vokey Spin Milled Wedges 46, 54, 60

Putter: Scotty Cameron Studio Select Fastback (Prototype) for Titleist

Ball: Titleist Pro V1x

Also Available
www.G2ent.co.uk

Also Available
www.G2ent.co.uk

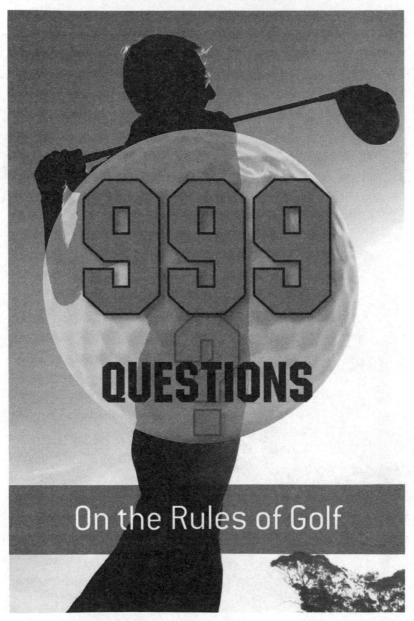

Also Available
www.G2ent.co.uk

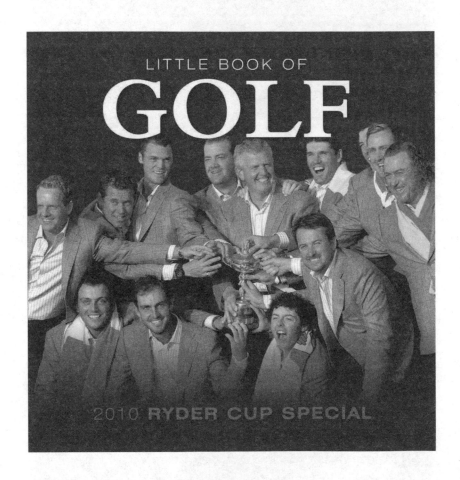

About the Author

Justin Doyle is a Sports Journalist with the Irish Sun newspaper. Residing in Virginia, County Cavan, he writes on Horse Racing as well as penning a weekly golf column entitled 'Fore'. He has also written in a freelance capacity for most of the major daily newspapers including the Irish Mirror, the Irish Mail and The Sunday Times.

'Rory' is his third major sports book. It follows on from his 2003 debut best-seller 'Misunderstood' – the autobiography of controversial GAA footballer Graham Geraghty. 'Pearl' followed in 2004. The story of Irish racehorse Florida Pearl, it was highly acclaimed with the Racing Post describing it as one of the best books ever written about a racehorse.